THE BIBLE IN THE MODERN WORLD

James Barr

THE BIBLE IN THE MODERN WORLD

SCM PRESS
London

TRINITY PRESS INTERNATIONAL
Philadelphia

First published 1973

Reissued 1990

SCM Press
26–30 Tottenham Road
London N1 4BZ

Trinity Press International
3725 Chestnut Street
Philadelphia, Pa. 19104

© James Barr 1973, 1990

Library of Congress Cataloging-in-Publication Data

Barr, James.
   The Bible in the modern world / James Barr.
      p. cm.
   Includes bibliographical references.
   ISBN 0–334–00113–7 : $12.95
      1. Bible—Evidences, authority, etc. 2. Bible—Inspiration.
   3. Bible—Hermeneutics. I. Title.
BS480.B354 1990
220.1–dc20   90–31632

ISBN 0–334–00113–7

Printed in Great Britain by
Richard Clay Ltd, Bungay, Suffolk

For Ellen Flesseman-van Leer

CONTENTS

PREFACE TO THE REISSUE

For this reissue, the text of the book has been left unchanged. Twenty years after the original writing, it would hardly have been possible to bring the work 'up to date' other than by writing an entirely new book, which would have dropped out of sight some of the earlier discussions and brought into the foreground some of the very large more recent literature. But the questionings and debates of the original time of writing are questionings and debates which have not disappeared from actuality; they are a stage through the problems of authority and relevance of the Bible.

Though some of the emphases of discussion have changed and some new interests have emerged, this book was in its own time, I think, mildly prophetic in its perception of these coming trends. Thus for example it is now widely felt that scholarship is moving from an older paradigm based upon history towards a newer paradigm based upon literature, and that shift of emphasis was already mirrored in these pages. Similarly, the interest in the *canonical* character of scripture has now greatly deepened, and would deserve a longer and more detailed treatment than it is given here; but this book already foresaw that some such development must follow from the course of earlier discussions. And, thirdly, the rising problem of fundamentalism, which, contrary to the hopes of many, had not been solved or overcome by the consensus of earlier twentieth-century theologies, and which has now, as we near the end of the century, come to be perhaps the most serious existential trouble of all religion, was already perceived and touched upon here. In all these respects I think I was already on the track of the developments that have in fact become most important.

Looking back over these years, I have been pleased and honoured by the good reception that the book has had. It has been widely used in discussion groups, ordination courses, and the like, and I believe it has met with, articulated and brought to expression many of the questions about scripture that most concern its readers today. I am very happy that this reissue will make it yet more widely available.

November 1989

James Barr

PREFACE

This book contains a series of Croall Lectures given in Edinburgh in November 1970. According to the rules laid down in the Settlement of the late John Croall, under which the lectures are conducted, 'The Lectures . . . shall be confined to the following subjects: – (First) The Evidences of Natural and Revealed Religion . . .' There then follow under the second and subsequent heads certain other subjects which might conceivably be attempted; but for our present purpose these can be ignored, and in undertaking to discuss the status of the Bible we are given confidence by the fact that that theme lies squarely within the first of the areas defined by Mr Croall. Whatever may be the position of natural religion, nothing is more certain than that the Bible has traditionally been taken as central or even unique among the evidences of revealed religion. We are therefore assured of the centrality of the subject within the traditional matter of theological study.

But while the subject itself is thus a somewhat traditional one, I trust that the argument of this book will not be equally traditional. The particular form of the title has been chosen because I want to discuss not the historical or the traditional views of the Bible and its place within Christianity but the problems which surround its status at the present day. Certain aspects which are historically important, such as the use of the Bible by the Reformers, have not been touched on at all, nor would my competence permit me to touch upon them.

Doubts about the competence of the author, indeed, may very justifiably be raised by this book. Professionally, I am a linguist and biblical scholar, and only a spare-time theologian. Professional theologians will observe in my argument gaps and amateurisms of all kinds. Of the total literature of the subject I have (thank God) read only a small proportion; though I did at one stage of my researches carry out an extensive study of conservative evangelical works, on which I then thought of concentrating. Most of all, in spite of my wish not to write a history, some historical remarks had to be included; and many of them include these vague terms, like 'in the early church' or 'up to modern times', if not even at worst 'long ago' or 'in the past', which must be the abomination of the true historian. Most of all I realize my poor knowledge in patristics and early church history, a field so vital for the formation and canonization of the Bible; of this I can only say that I aspire to learn more.

If I ask myself why I have taken up the subject at all, one reason is that a book needs to be written. Though the subject is a central one, the existing books on it in English arise from a rather different situation and some valuable ones are out of print. My aim has not been to give definitive answers but to provide a survey and discussion of the question which will be adequate until something better is written. From time to time I am beset with fears that the position I set out has something wrong with it which I do not perceive. I have not however allowed such fears to trouble me too much. As I see it, in such matters it is not our vocation to be right, but to say what we think as hard and clear as we can. Others can then make the replies and the corrections that are needed. While mentioning other books, I should add that J. Wirsching's *Was ist schriftgemäß?* (1971) had not appeared when the lectures were given and was available to me only in the last stages of revision for publication.

The other reason why I have taken up the subject lies in my own experience and in the encouragement given me by friends. Problems of the status of the Bible have been with me since I first became interested in theology; and no one can teach Old Testament to theological students over a good number of years without being forced to reflect on the subject. My work on it in recent years has been within the context of the ecumenical studies on hermeneutics and later on biblical authority, both in the British group and in international meetings; these studies have been a stimulus to continued thinking, in a field where I do no regular teaching.

I had however given lectures and taken part in discussions on the subject over several years before the giving of the Croall Lectures in Edinburgh. Elements from the Smyth Lectures, given in Columbia Theological Seminary, Decatur, Georgia, in October 1964, have been re-thought and have contributed to the position here maintained. I remember with special gratitude the discussions with colleagues and students in New Zealand and Australia in 1968.

Special mention is due also to two American colloquia which honoured me with an invitation to take part: the Pittsburgh Festival on the Gospels in 1970 and the colloquium at Union Theological Seminary, Richmond, Virginia, in 1971, in which the group of articles published in *Interpretation* xxv was taken as a basis for discussion.

Going further back, I acknowledge the stimulus of two other American colloquia which particularly studied Catholic-Protestant relations: that at Harvard in 1963 (reported on in the volume *Ecumenical Dialogue at Harvard: the Roman Catholic-Protestant Colloquium*, Harvard, 1964) and that at Notre Dame in 1964. Despite all that I owe to these discussions, I have not in this book tried to develop in any detail the discussion between Roman Catholic and non-Roman Catholic views about scripture, and this I regret; but I have not been able to keep up with the literature of the subject, and my knowledge of recent developments in Roman Catholic theology is too weak. I rejoice, however, that it was possible to approach the subject at all in an atmosphere in which the Roman Catholic/Protestant opposition, so long central to all.discussion, can at least in part be left on one side. That it is possible to proceed at all without being burdened with this opposition is a happy augury.

Protestant conservatism and fundamentalism has been mentioned rather more. This is not out of a wish to engage in debate with that point of view or to provide a full analysis of it, though this might well be desirable; it is rather because the heritage of this older biblicism is, at least in our Anglo-Saxon culture, so strong that it influences almost all talk about the Bible, not least among those who most seek to depart from its point of view.

The position within Judaism, though seldom explicitly mentioned, is also often in my mind; and many problems met by Christians in their use of the Bible are problems for Jewish readers also. The sharing of the Hebrew Bible by Jews and Christians alike is something which is continually in my thoughts. If this book speaks mainly of 'Christian' faith and of 'Christian' questions about the Bible, this is not because I wish to ignore the questions in the form in which they are met by Jews, but because I do not think it my business to tell Jewish readers how they should read or what they should think.

As for the plan of the book, the first six chapters are more or less analysis and critique of the problem as it stands today, plus some hints of possible answers; the seventh chapter presents what seems to me the foundation for a possible position in its essentials, and what follows is intended to explicate this position and gather together its implications.

Finally, I have to thank the trustees of the Croall Lectureship Trust for honouring me with their invitation to deliver these lectures, and the teaching staff and students of New College, Edinburgh, for coming to listen to them with careful attention at a time when they were even more incoherent in form and uncertain in final outcome than they now are. The experience of giving them, and that not least in the setting of the college where I was myself a student and later a professor, was a stimulus towards the rethinking of them for publication. But most of all I am grateful to the friends with whom I have worked in so many discussions on these matters, and whose friendship has encouraged me to persevere with them: Dr Ellen Flesseman-van Leer, to whom this book is dedicated, Dr Dennis Nineham, Professor Christopher Evans, Professor Dietrich Ritschl, and others. Professor Evans has greatly helped me with criticism and advice on my typescript, and John Bowden of the SCM Press has done much more than a publisher's duty in furnishing valuable suggestions.

July 1972 J.B.

I

HOW WE REACHED OUR
PRESENT SITUATION

1. *The post-war consensus*

In the years following the Second World War the importance
attached to the Bible in Christian faith and thought was very high,
perhaps as high as it had ever been for a century or more. Wide
circles in the churches and in theology seemed to have agreed that
the Bible was of absolutely central importance and that it could not
be neglected without disaster to the church and to the faith of
Christians. The centrality of the Bible seemed to be accepted and
acclaimed by many features in the current theology and in the
practical life of the churches.

Much of the theology of the time emphasized the Bible very
strongly. This emphasis is most marked in the movement often
known as 'neo-orthodox', best exemplified in Karl Barth. Taking
its rise soon after the First World War, by the end of the Second
this movement had made a great impact. Its emphasis was strongly
biblical: it stressed the God of the Bible, the God who revealed
himself as he was, the God of Israel, the concepts and the thought
of the Bible. In this it looked back to, and revered, the Reformation. It rejected the 'liberal' types of theology which were – it was
alleged – rather a human attempt to see and understand God in the
image of man, and which had all too strongly stressed man and his
culture, man and his thinking. Faith begins with the God who
speaks, and it is the Bible that testifies to this God.

There were many – and especially so in the English-speaking
world – who did not accept the particular arguments of theologians
like Barth. The impact of the neo-orthodox movement was diffuse
and general; this does not alter the fact that it was substantial.

More correctly, perhaps, we should not speak of the impact of neo-orthodoxy on theology as a whole; rather, neo-orthodoxy was an acute symptom of a tendency which was widespread in all theology. Powerful currents of theological thought, even if they disagreed with the specific neo-orthodox positions, found themselves moving closer to the Bible, depending more heavily upon it, emphasizing it and its distinctiveness more strongly. There was a trend towards the primacy of revelation, and a corresponding down-grading of 'natural theology' or 'natural religion', or indeed of 'religion' altogether. It became common to make a strong contrast between the thought of the Bible, which was theologically positive, and competing modes of thinking, such as the Greek and philosophi-cal strain in our cultural heritage, which in comparison were treated negatively. There were indeed always those who criticized these tendencies; but these tendencies were very strong and those who opposed them often found themselves forced on to the defensive.

Meanwhile some of the difficult problems about the Bible, which had plagued the churches, and especially the Protestant churches, for over a century, seemed to be approaching some kind of a solu-tion. For over a century critical scholars had been using historical methods on the biblical books, and these methods had greatly altered the estimate in which these books were generally held. By applying to them the same methods of historical criticism which were applied to (let us say) the works of ancient historians or annalists, scholars had come to assert (a) that many biblical books were not written by the persons to whom they were traditionally attributed; (b) that on the contrary they might be made up of layers of material from different periods, put together by a com-piler at the end of the process; (c) that they contained, or might contain, elements of myth or historical legend, so that the real history of the times had to be reconstructed and could not be read off from the surface text of the Bible.

These critical views occasioned profound splits within Pro-testantism. To a conservative wing they appeared to damage or to deny the centrality and authority of the Bible within the church; if it was historically inaccurate, how could it be theologically depend-able? The more liberal types of theology, on the other hand, leant less heavily on the Bible, and tended to make a very selective use of it. The historical scholars, for their part, seemed to many to pro-ceed with their analytic work while caring nothing either for any synthetic view of the Bible or for any constructive view of its importance or authority. The resultant splits within Protestantism between a more biblical conservatism and a wide-ranging liberalism were for a long time the cause of a deep agony.

The position reached about the end of the Second World War appeared, however, to overcome some of this difficulty. The emphasis upon the Bible which the newer theology upheld did not imply any kind of fundamentalism or obscurantism; on the contrary, it claimed to be compatible with a full acceptance of modern methods of historical research. Indeed, the biblical revival within theology – for such it was – included within itself a strong element of polemic against fundamentalism and biblicistic conservatism, which it accused of maintaining the form of biblical authority while failing to appreciate its own inner logic. Thus, even where it most strongly reacted against the 'liberal' criticism of the preceding generations, the newer view of the Bible claimed to accept as legitimate a fully 'critical' reading of the Bible. It seemed possible, then, to be biblical without being reactionary; indeed, biblical thinking was seen as something novel, liberating and revolutionary.

One aspect of the thinking of the post-war period was its insistence that the Bible could and should be treated 'as a whole'. This was an aspect of the reaction against the liberal theologies, which had often seemed to absolutize one element in the Bible, such as the Synoptic picture of Jesus (or parts of that picture), and which had thus played off Jesus against Paul or the God of the Old Testament against that of the New. It was also a reaction against the purely analytic procedure of biblical critics: granted, it was argued, that the Bible can be split up into different sources, can not after all that say something about the sense of the whole? It was freely admitted that historical differences and varieties of emphasis existed within the totality of the Bible; but these were different voices which formed a harmonious choir. The Bible had its effect on Christian faith not through one part or another but through the way in which all the parts and elements interrelated. Thus, to take one of the most striking instances, it was axiomatic that the Old Testament belonged together with the New; and those tendencies within liberal theology which had neglected the Old Testament were severely condemned. The 'Hebrew way of thinking' not only animated the entire Old Testament but ran throughout the New also; indeed, some said that it was the key to the right understanding of the latter. The New Testament, it was argued, could be totally misunderstood if it was read through contemporary Greek categories; only if it was read in Hebrew terms could it be rightly comprehended. Thus the assurance of the unity of the Bible now stood at its highest point for decades. The analytic effect of biblical criticism, which had broken down the ancient harmonizations and revealed the diversity of sources (diversity both in their historical accuracy and in their theological emphasis), was now balanced by a more synthetic approach.

Such an assurance about the Bible had important effects on practical activity. There was a renewed emphasis on preaching, with biblical exposition at its centre. There was, indeed, much uncertainty about the attempt to put into effect the principle of 'biblical preaching' and, especially in the English-speaking world, a modern homiletic approach built upon biblical exposition never really became clear. Nevertheless some considerable movement in favour of a more biblical type of preaching certainly took place.

Meanwhile the ecumenical movement was one of the centres of activity in the churches, and here also the revived biblical emphasis had great effects. It was believed that the Bible was the element common to all Christianity and that as the various churches and traditions grew closer to the Bible they would also find themselves growing closer to one another. There were serious disagreements between the different Christian traditions; but these differences, it could be supposed, might be traced to different cultural, philosophical or otherwise non-biblical traditions, adopted in the course of historical development. It was thought that the contrast with biblical thinking would identify these other traditions for what they were, and that they would thus come to be purged away or at least subjugated to dominant biblical patterns; if this happened, the churches would find themselves closer together. The practice of common biblical exegesis thus formed an important part of the agenda of ecumenical discussion.

Such discussion also included the many social and political questions which came before the churches. Here too the biblical emphasis was felt to be positive. It seemed to make the life of the churches more open to the world, to its human and material problems; it seemed to make Christians conscious of material and practical realities and less concentrated upon spiritual or ideal entities. This was part of the appeal and attractiveness of the biblical message; and, correspondingly, it was to the Bible that men and churches had recourse in their search for answers. It was considered at least possible to search for a 'biblical view' of work, or of health, or of the state, and considerable study was devoted to such quests.

In all these ways, then, the Bible seemed in the post-war period to have returned to a position of calm, assured and creative centrality within the churches and the faith of Christians. There had indeed been some severe buffeting at the time when historical criticism began; there had also been some disdain or neglect under the reign of liberal theology; there were still indeed questions which had to be settled. But the central and essential place of the Bible in Christian faith and in the life of the churches seemed now to be widely accepted and secure.[1] Few or none were aware that the place of the Bible was soon to be challenged again and that questions which had been thought settled were to be raised again in even more acute ways than before.

2. Recent questionings

The situation I have sketched existed up to about ten years ago; and from the early sixties onwards the climate of theology has drastically changed. The strongly authoritative type of theology, with its centre in the primacy of revelation and its most developed representative in neo-orthodoxy, has lost its impetus and its leadership. Philosophical theology, as distinct from biblically-based theology, has again increased in influence. Ideas which had been regarded as belonging to outmoded 'liberalism' are being freely discussed once again. It sometimes seems as if the great neo-orthodox revolution in theology had not taken place at all, so many of its favourite positions are denied or simply ignored. The reasons for this lie beyond the scope of this present enquiry; but the following points, which are aspects of this same shift of theological climate, may also suggest some reasons why that shift took place.

For one thing, it is felt that we have not yet reached the bottom of the problems posed for theology by modern methods of studying the Bible, for example by historical criticism and by the study of

[1] When in the remainder of this book I use the phrase 'the modern revival of biblical authority' I refer to the situation which has just been described.

contacts between the Bible and other religions. The post-war consensus, if we may so call it, *permitted* such methods of study to exist but did not allow them to have decisive weight. Neoorthodoxy, as we now see it, stood much closer to biblical conservatism than its claims at the time might have suggested. Today it is widely felt that a more positive theological value for the whole range of scholarly techniques, as biblical scholars in fact apply them, needs to be worked out and stated.

Secondly, there is less confidence in the idea that the Bible must be read 'as a whole'. There are those who feel, on the contrary, that the diversity and disagreement found within the Bible is a more sure characteristic of its nature and a more promising clue to its meaning. The attempt to make 'Hebrew thought' a guide to the coherence of the Bible has been discredited. If the emphasis on the Bible 'as a whole' grew up in reaction against the purely analytic interests of scholars, so in turn the strivings after synthesis in post-war exegesis ended up by seeming like old-fashioned harmonization and made people turn again with relief to analysis as a fresher approach. Once again, therefore, we find that people are giving different values to different parts of the Bible. This affects not least the position of the Old Testament. To neo-orthodox theologians like Barth it was simply axiomatic that the Old and the New Testaments belonged together in respect of authority; anyone who doubted this was merely stating that he did not belong to the historic Christian faith, built upon the foundation of prophets and apostles. Today, by contrast, we are once again meeting with a considerable tendency to grade the Old Testament lower than the New.[2]

Thirdly, as for the ideal of biblical and expository preaching, quite unabashed reactions against it can be found:

> I often preach without a text or on a text from a non-biblical writer, Kierkegaard for example, or even on occasions Katherine Whitehorn![3]

[2] On the special problems of this, see my article 'The Old Testament and the new Crisis of Biblical Authority', *Interpretation* xxv (1971), pp. 24–40; cf. also below, pp. 114–7, 164–7.

[3] Nineham, *BJRL* lii (1969), p. 193. For those who do not understand the allusion, Katherine Whitehorn is a writer with a weekly column on women's affairs and social and moral questions generally, in the British Sunday newspaper *The Observer*.

The task of the church, it is suggested, is to say what it believes today, and not to expound the text of an ancient document. The Church does not speak, and never has spoken, on the basis of any authority external to itself, and it deludes itself if it imagines that it does so. Christian speech works from what one person believes today and appeals to what others today may also believe or accept. In such a process it is entirely incidental whether a biblical passage is taken as starting-point or 'authority' or not. Dr Nineham continues the passage just quoted as follows:[4]

> And I have to admit to myself that the spirit of my sermons is very much that expressed in Leonard Hodgson's formula: 'This is how *I* see it; can you not see it like that as well?'[5]

As for the ecumenical discussion, the World Council of Churches became aware of a widespread dissatisfaction, especially among biblical scholars, with the way in which the Bible had been used in the ecumenical study documents of the post-war decades. At the worst, this dissatisfaction reached the point of a considerable alienation between scholarly exegetes and ecumenical theologians. This fact was one main reason why a fresh ecumenical study of biblical authority was undertaken.[6] Within that study we see a retreat from the idea that the Bible is the one common and unifying element possessed by the divided churches:

> The assumption that all churches have the Bible in common is ambiguous until the question of authority has been clarified, and the hope that common exegetical work might be the way to a common understanding of Christian truth has been seen to be naive, or at least premature.[7]

[4] Nineham, ibid.

[5] Cf. L. Hodgson in *On the Authority of the Bible*, p. 10, where however the reference is to scholarly discussion rather than to preaching; but Hodgson may well have used the same phrase in a variety of connections.

[6] The study document prepared for the initation of this study is in *The Ecumenical Review* xxi (1969), pp. 135–66. On this particular point see p. 137, para. (c) (ii), and on the 'unity' of the Bible para. (c) (i).

[7] *The Ecumenical Review*, ibid., p. 138, para. (c) (iv). The final report of the study, *Louvain 1971*, does however rather reiterate the very position which was initially questioned: 'We must [*sic*] first realize that the Bible is the common point of reference for all Christians and all Churches. It is the basis of their faith and the rule of their conduct . . .' (*Louvain 1971*, p. 9).

One of the factors which probably contributed to the fresh uncertainty about the status of the Bible was the discussion about hermeneutics or methods of interpretation, which was very active in theological circles in the later fifties and the sixties. The World Council of Churches study on authority itself grew out of a previous study of the hermeneutical discussion;[8] that study seemed in its outcome to call for and to lead naturally on to an exploration of biblical authority. More generally, the emphasis laid on the discussion of interpretative methods seemed to reduce the possibility of any simple reliance on the authority of the Bible. To put it at its simplest, if the Bible when interpreted in one way gave a quite different impression from the Bible when interpreted in another way, then the Bible in itself could hardly be taken as a decisive authority. Into the ramifications of this question we need not go at this point; let it suffice that as a matter of historical fact the discussion of hermeneutics probably constituted a pathway which led from the greater assurance about biblical authority, which prevailed in the earlier post-war period, to the greater uncertainty which prevails today.

From all these points of view, then, we seem in comparison with the recent past to have returned to a situation in which the status and value of the Bible is very much in question. Moreover, such a situation may well come to be permanent. During the revival of biblical authority one might have supposed that acceptance of the Bible constituted normality and that questioning of its authority had been a temporary (though painful) interruption of the normal state of affairs. The speedy loss of this confidence makes us wonder whether the opposite may now be the case, and whether questioning and doubt about the status of the Bible may come to be normal in the life of the churches.

It is important however not to exaggerate the extent of this questioning of the status of the Bible. In the first place, it appears to vary very much in extent between different national and cultural settings. The most radical questioning seems to have appeared in English-speaking theology, both in Great Britain and in the United States. According to my impression, which is of course limited, there is uncertainty also in continental theology; but it is rather uncertainty about the *mode* of biblical authority, about the way in

[8] See *New Directions in Faith and Order: Bristol 1967*, pp. 32–41, 106f., 151f.; *The Ecumenical Review*, ibid., esp. pp. 135–39.

which it is to be understood. In English-speaking theology one hears the more radical question: why should we affirm at all anything so strange as 'biblical authority'? Why should this collection of old books have any more influence over us than another lot of books, and why should it have more importance than all sorts of perceptions which we gain from other sources, both ancient and modern, written and unwritten? For this radical questioning of the status of the Bible, historical and cultural reasons might be suggested: is it the effect of empiricist philosophy? or does it result from the slight and brief influence of neo-orthodox theology in some English-speaking countries, notably England herself? or is it to be traced to the thin tradition of expository preaching in Anglicanism, to the rhetorical and often personality-centred pulpit oratory of Presbyterianism? or does it belong to the libertarian style of Anglo-Saxon social philosophy? Between these explanations, fortunately, we do not here require to make a choice. The questions which are being asked deserve to have an answer, whatever the cultural background from which they have arisen.

Secondly, however, we should not give the impression that English-speaking theology had suddenly risen in massed rebellion against the centrality of the Bible. This would be entirely untrue. The majority of influential theologians would seem to refrain from any outspoken questioning of the status of the Bible. Indeed, many modern theologians appear to be able to work without giving much thought to its status at all. One of the difficulties is that the present uncertainties about the Bible do not attach themselves to any one clearly formulated position worked out by competent theologians. These uncertainties are voiced only by a few scholars and are not made very articulate by them. Nevertheless they represent something very real and present at the grassroots of English-speaking Christianity. They are part of an ethos, a generally diffused temperament; and part of this ethos is shared also by those large segments of English-speaking Christianity which maintain a more traditional position towards the Bible.

It is amongst the younger people that uncertainties about the Bible are most felt: felt among the younger clergy, and often among the more progressive members of it; and, as with so many other things today, felt among the students. It is asked: Why so much study of the Bible? Can it have much relevance for our needs today? Would not a social study of contemporary society, a discussion of present philosophical trends, a course in psychology, offer us more? On all sides one hears reports of theological students who have lost interest in biblical study and prefer to develop psychological and sociological interests; this last is certainly not an English-speaking phenomenon only, but seems on the contrary to be even more marked in some continental countries.

We recognize, then, that serious questionings about the place of the Bible in the life and faith of the churches exist. However, whether these are more vaguely felt by students or more expertly expressed by theologians, it would be wrong to categorize them as a 'rejection' of the Bible and of its value. To those who hold more traditional views of the Bible, indeed, these questionings may seem to amount to rejection; but, as seen from the viewpoint of the askers of questions, nothing so definite, so explicit, so self-conscious and so clearly negative is intended. We are not dealing with a worked-out doctrine which 'denies the authority of the Bible', but with something vaguer and more intangible. If we try to analyse this, some of the elements which emerge are as follows:

(i) Questions about *relevance*: The problems of our own time are very different from those of biblical times; how then can material from that very different biblical situation be decisive for our problems?

(ii) Questions about *communicability*: There are very deep differences in culture and thought between the men of the Bible and ourselves; how then can we expect that which was meaningful to them to communicate the same meaning to us?

(iii) Questions about *limitations*: The Bible is a limited set of books, chosen partly by accident and coming from a limited segment in the total history of the church; how can its insights be decisive for us in any way which is qualitatively different from that which attaches to other books and other times?

(iv) Questions about *isolation*: How can the Bible be assigned a position qualitatively different from all the other factors which come into the mind of the Christian, or the mind of the church, when decisions about faith and ethics have to be taken?

(v) Questions about *our responsibility*: The task of the church is to say what the church and Christians believe today. This responsibility is evaded or distorted if we suppose that our main responsibility is to restate, to reinterpret, or to make our thoughts dependent upon, what was believed by the men of biblical times.

Such then, if my analysis is right, are some features of the present questioning of the place of the Bible in Christian life and faith. In general, these questions do not form an outright negation of more traditional views of the Bible. Only sometimes do they question or oppose the older views outright; sometimes they fasten on weak points in them; but most commonly they tend to outflank the traditional views rather than to clash with them head-on. Thus the focus of the whole problem has come to be different from what it was in an earlier time, and this is a main reason why the discussion has to be taken up afresh. Little can be expected from a mere reiteration of the arguments used in that earlier time; these arguments are already familiar to at least some of the questioners of today, and indeed it is the very familiarity of them, and the constant reiteration of them, which has caused them to lose conviction and made them into a source of irritation.

The situation then is somewhat as follows. We have a great central body of people in the churches who attribute a high status and authority to the Bible, but who also suffer a considerable uncertainty about this, an uncertainty which has been increasing during the last ten or fifteen years, as the glow of the post-war biblical revival in theology has faded. On their 'left' is a much smaller but important group, which is more actively questioning the status still generally allotted to the Bible. On their 'right', on the other hand, stands the phenomenon of conservative Protestant and fundamentalist Christianity, which upholds traditional views of the Bible and appears – at least at first sight – to offer a clear and unshaking testimony to its authority. It is not my purpose in this book to engage in a debate with fundamentalist opinion,[9] but reference has to be made to it from time to time. Any treatment of the Bible has to provide some demarcation of the borders with fundamentalism, and this in particular for two reasons: (a) in the public eye the fundamentalist point of view often appears as the genuine manifestation of what a truly *biblical* Christianity would have to be; and (b) a great deal of discussion of the Bible among people who are not fundamentalist is bedevilled by the use of categories and arguments which would be appropriate only if the parties were in fact thinking in fundamentalist terms. But apart from this, this book is written on the assumption that for its readers

[9] For a brief treatment of the subject, see my *Old and New in Interpretation*, pp. 201–6.

– as for the mainstream of modern Christian faith – real dogmatic fundamentalism is not a live option.

In approaching these problems, it will be useful to consider here some leading concepts which have been used in order to express the place of the Bible in relation to the church and the Christian, to doctrine and to faith. To this preliminary examination of concepts the next chapter will be devoted.

II

SOME LEADING CONCEPTS

1. Inspiration

To the average layman, no doubt this is the term which is most likely to be applied to the Bible: it is 'inspired', it somehow comes from God, what is in it is true, it does not contain falsehood. Among theologians, however, the term 'inspiration' has not been very much used in modern times. The areas of its continuing use have been at the two opposite ends of the spectrum: in Roman Catholic theology on the one hand, and in Protestant fundamentalism on the other. Just because the word is so associated with fundamentalism, other trends of non-Roman theology have tended to avoid it. Thus the term has been definitely out of fashion: the World Council of Churches study found it a 'surprise' that they were led to think of it.[1]

If we use the term 'inspiration', the result is that we emphasize the *origin* of the Bible. It comes from God, and this differentiates it from other writings, which are the work of men. But *in what way* does scripture come from God? In what way can he be thought to have inspired it? This is one of the thorniest problems of any idea of biblical inspiration.

It is not difficult to give a probable historical account of the roots of the idea. It goes back, we may suggest, to the Old Testament picture of a God who was a *speaking* God, who used intelligible and articulate language with a grammar the same as that of human speakers. But not only did God himself thus speak in articulate language; he also had agents who spoke for him, and the words which they spoke were words which God was believed to have given them to speak. The most central among such agents

[1] *Louvain 1971*, p. 20.

were the prophets; in some traditions they were regarded as having received the Spirit of God, and it was through this that these human agents spoke not their own ideas but that which God had to say. Ideas of this kind, belonging to a significant stratum within the Bible, were perhaps in due course extended and made to apply to all sacred scripture. Yet the term 'inspired', though it appears in the Bible itself, does so only in a late and marginal document (II Tim. 3.16). Even there its scope and syntax may be variously interpreted: contrast the AV with its 'All scripture is given by inspiration of God, and is profitable for doctrine . . .' and the NEB with its 'Every inspired scripture has its use for teaching the truth . . .' It is an open question which books or documents were included within 'scripture' by the writer of II Timothy, and an open question also what was implied in his mind by 'inspired', what it involved and what it excluded.

As I have said, 'inspiration' has been a central term in Protestant fundamentalism. Here the emphasis on the *origin* of scripture is maintained, though it is doubtful whether fundamentalists are very clear about the *mode* of inspiration, any more than other people are. In fundamentalist opinion inspiration is particularly linked with *infallibility* or *inerrancy*. The point then is that the Bible, being from God, cannot be wrong; it cannot be in error and cannot lead into error.

'Error' here means both of two things, historical error and theological error. If the Bible reports something as a historical fact, then it is a true historical fact. For instance, if it describes a Daniel who lived at the time of Nebuchadnezzar and Darius, then there was such a Daniel and he did the things described. The historical-critical view, that the book was written long after the time of these kings, is to be rejected because it is linked with the notion that the stories in question are largely legendary.

Secondly, there is no theological error in the Bible; what it teaches about faith and morals is absolutely right and has to be accepted. Naturally, there are questions of balance between one element and another; even fundamentalist Christians do not consider every element equally binding. Problems of interpretation exist for most fundamentalists as for other people; but, once this is taken into consideration, the Bible is theologically infallible. You may not know the true interpretation; but you know that, when it is found, the text rightly interpreted will be absolutely right.

It is characteristic of fundamentalism that it makes these two elements, the historical and the theological, interdependent in a particular way. The fundamentalist denies that there is any historical error in the Bible; he does this because he feels that, if any historical error were admitted, it would open the way to assertions of theological error as well. His characteristic argument is 'Where do you stop?' If the Bible is 'wrong' about the age of Ishmael when he was expelled with his mother from Abraham's camp, or about the historicity of Daniel, then it can be wrong about the love of God or about justification by faith. I shall not pursue this argument here; I wish only to point out that through widespread use in fundamentalism such connotations have become attached to the term 'inspiration'. For the average English speaker this word has come to mean infallibility, the absence of error.

A second association which in the minds of many has come to be built into the term 'inspiration' is an emphasis on the literal, the verbal. The phrase 'verbal inspiration', though not always quite clear, seems to imply that the Bible is not only inspired in its general purport, in its ideas or its message, but that the verbal form itself, the exact sequence of words and sentences, is inspired by God (and therefore, as we have seen, free from error). A sign of this among fundamentalists is the love for the very wording of the Bible, a tendency to argue by quoting its exact verbal form, an impression therefore given that the biblical text can be applied *direct* to the answering of questions in faith and ethics. Even among fundamentalists, indeed, there are many shades of opinion about the exact extent of verbal inspiration, or about the notion of an inspiration that is not quite verbal but comes close to it. We shall later have something more to say about the verbal form of scripture and about literalism in the interpretation of it. But for the general public the effect, which we note for the present, is that the term 'inspiration' is completely tied up with a concentration on the verbal form and detail of the Bible.

As has been mentioned, the concept of inspiration has been much used in Roman Catholicism as well as in conservative Protestantism; but it has been more creatively and flexibly handled in Roman theology, doubtless because in it scripture is only one of the basic theological norms (tradition being the other) and not the sole such norm (as in conservative Protestantism). Within Roman theology there has therefore been a potential for a more open use of the term; but this potential has not been well realized. The nineteenth century was a time when Protestantism was agonized by the conflict between the newer historical methods and the older inspirational dogma. In this time it would have been possible for Rome to accept fully the new types of knowledge, and to say that they would do no damage to the basic theological tradition of the church. Rome, however, apparently out of sheer conservatism, then burdened itself with a series of rigidly backward rulings which have been a source of difficulty to Roman Catholic scholars until very recent times. Hans Küng[2] gives the following account of the matter:

> The Tridentine decree makes no mention of the inerrancy of the Bible as a result of inspiration. It was only in Protestantism that the theory of literal inspiration was rigorously maintained and systematically developed. It was only towards the end of the nineteenth century that the popes, under the pressure of destructive critical exegesis, took over the theory of literal inspiration worked out by Protestant Orthodoxy, at a time when it was strangely out of phase . . . From the time of Leo XIII, and particularly during the modernist crisis, the complete and absolute inerrancy of Scripture was explicitly and systematically maintained in papal encyclicals.

Thus in fact the close association between inspiration and inerrancy, which has been so evident in Protestantism, has been found in Roman Catholicism also. Nevertheless anyone who wished to revive the term 'inspiration' for modern use would be likely to look for guidance towards the Roman tradition. Is it likely, however, that such a revival might take place? Certainly the link with inerrancy would have to be broken. Theologically this is not difficult: why should God not have inspired a scripture with errors in it, through which he might nevertheless truly communicate with men? The Gospels themselves, after all, are full of parables, which are fictions. All this can be argued. But as a matter of practical semantics it is not easy to get rid of the burden which past history has loaded upon such a word.

There is indeed another linguistic tradition in the use of 'inspiration' to which we could conceivably turn. Rather than the more theological use of the word, we could consider its use with reference to *poetic* or *literary* inspiration. This conception would suggest not

[2] H. Küng, *Infallible? An Enquiry* (London: Collins, 1971), p. 174.

so much historical or theological accuracy, inerrancy and infallibility, but rather sublimity, profundity of insight, existential
power of communication. Coleridge's dictum that 'Whatever finds
me, bears witness for itself that it has proceeded from a Holy
Spirit' would be an instance of such a softer meaning of inspiration.
Moreover, it is likely that the general literary sense of 'inspiration'
has always been somewhat in the background when the theological
sense has been used. Nevertheless the theological sense of the word,
in spite of its probable contacts with the literary sense, has generally
gone so far beyond that latter sense that most people now are little
aware of a connection between them. The substance of this question, however, will come before us again when we consider the
Bible as literature and the Bible as information; and it may suffice
for the present that we have simply mentioned it.

Whether the *word* 'inspiration' can be revitalized for use today
or not, it stands for something that seems to be necessary in a
Christian account of the status of the Bible. It expresses the belief,
which most Christians surely hold, that in some way the Bible
comes from God, that he has in some sense a part in its origin, that
there is a linkage between the basic mode through which he has
communicated with man and the coming into existence of this body
of literature.

It is here however that we come to the most serious problems of
the idea of inspiration, once conceptions of infallibility and inerrancy have been got out of the way. *In what way* does one suppose
God to have inspired the scripture? The phrase 'in some way',
which I used above, is typical of our thinking about this subject.
Even for fundamentalists this is an uncertain area, and for the
majority of modern Christians it is a field of blank ignorance. We
do not have any idea of ways in which God might straightforwardly
communicate articulate thoughts or sentences to men; it just
doesn't happen. Or do we suppose that the men of the Bible thought
their own thoughts and that God – by his Spirit, shall we say? –
somehow guided them? Note again the word 'somehow'.

A modern view would, I think, have to abandon the traditional
models used for the understanding of these problems. These
models include in particular: (a) a special mode of direct communication from God to persons like prophets; (b) cessation of this
special mode at more or less the end of the biblical period. Today I
think we believe, or have to believe, that God's communication

with the men of the biblical period was not on any different terms from the mode of his communication with his people today. 'Inspiration' would then mean that the God whom we worship was also likewise in contact with his people in ancient times, and that in their particular circumstances, in the stage in which they existed, he was present in the formation of their tradition and in the crystallization of that tradition as a scripture; but that the mode of this contact was not different from the mode in which God has continued to make himself known to men. Not many theologians seem to have formulated their views on this question; but I do not see how else we can think in the present day.

To these questions we shall later return. For the present our purpose is simply to make a preliminary exploration of the concepts through which the status of the Bible has been formulated. We have looked at some of the associations of 'inspiration', its scope and its limitations; and we now pass on to another traditional formulation.

2. The Word of God

In the last section we observed that the main stream of non-Roman theology in this century has somewhat neglected the idea of inspiration. With the idea of 'the Word of God' the reverse is the case, and this concept has been carefully and elaborately discussed, most notably in the theology of Karl Barth, which has indeed at times been characterized as a theology of the Word of God. Without attempting an exact historical exposition of his views, I shall outline the sort of general position which would be recognized as Barthian.

The average English speaker once again, if consulted about the meaning of terms, might say that 'the Word of God' implies the same about the Bible as 'inspiration' does; it would mean that the Bible comes from God, is the ultimate expression of his will, is without any kind of error. According to a more sophisticated current of theology, this is entirely wrong. God in his revealing reveals himself. He reveals himself in his Word, and that Word is Jesus Christ. In essence, therefore, and primarily, the Word of God is not the Bible; rather, it is Jesus Christ himself; it is in him, according to St John's Gospel, that the Word is incarnate.

This does not mean that Jesus Christ, the Word of God, can be understood or approached apart from the Bible. One may state the relation by using the idea of witness or testimony. The Bible is the essential witness to Jesus Christ; it is the testimony of those who were witnesses to him. The testimony points not to itself but to that of which it speaks. Thus the real revelatory content is not the Bible itself, but the person and acts to which it testifies. The Bible is not a revealed book, for God does not reveal books, chapters, sentences and verses, but reveals himself. It is wrong therefore to say that the Bible is revelation; it is only witness to revelation.

But though it is a human witness, the Bible is also a necessary witness. It is necessary because of the way in which God's revelation took place: not through universally attainable ideas, but through historical events. God made himself known through a definite series of events at a particular time and place in history; this being so, a record is indispensable if access is to be had to this revelation. And the Bible is not only a necessary witness, it is also a fitting and appropriate witness. It is not a mere historical record but a response in faith; and the writers are not mere objective witnesses of external events but are men who believe that God has spoken to them through these events. Thus, though the Word of God is not identical with the Bible, the Bible is an essential and appropriate access to the Word of God, and one cannot hope to hear the Word of God except through the mediation of the Bible.

This being so, it is not inappropriate that the Bible should also be termed 'the Word of God', though it is not the Word of God in the primary sense of that term. One way in which Barth expressed this was the idea that the Word of God had a threefold form. The primary form of the Word of God was Jesus Christ himself, the revealed Word. The secondary form was the written scripture, the written Word; and the third form was the word of the church's proclamation, the preached Word. All of these were linked. The Word in the primary sense, Jesus Christ, speaks only as he is witnessed to by the scripture and proclaimed in faith by the church. The Bible is Word of God only through its function of witness to God in his self-revelation; and it is Word of God only as it is received in faith and proclaimed in the church. The preaching of the church is Word of God only in so far as it is truly subservient to the Word of God in Jesus Christ and to the biblical witness thereto.

Another thought which often appears in association with these is the thought of the scripture not *being* but *becoming* the Word of God. It is not a solid and static entity, identical with the Word of God; it is something which can become dynamic and alive, and then *becomes* the Word of God. This is another, somewhat more existentialist, picture of a unity between the Bible and the Word of God which is still not an identity. Similarly, one can speak of scripture 'becoming the Gospel'; in the words of a modern Roman Catholic writer:[3]

> Thus Scripture is invested with authority, the authority of God, only by becoming the Gospel. The question then is to know how Scripture effectively becomes the Gospel.

Yet another thought which belongs to the same circle of ideas is the view that the Bible has two aspects, one divine and one human. The person of Christ, as understood in traditional christology, is taken as an analogy. He is both truly God and truly man; and correspondingly the Bible is both Word of God and Word of Man. These terms are not alternative but co-extensive. It is not intended to mean that parts are divine and parts are human, any more than parts of Christ were divine and other parts human. The entire Bible is human word, subject to the strains, weaknesses and errors of any human product; in this respect it stands no higher than any other book and deserves, indeed requires, to be studied with just the same methods as any other. But the entire Bible is also divine Word; it has something to say that does not arise from human

---

[3] R. Marlé, *Ecumenical Review* xxi (1969), p. 159; cf. also E. Käsemann, *New Testament Questions of Today* (London: SCM Press, 1969), p. 271: 'The Bible is therefore for Paul in no way, in itself and apart from its use, Gospel. But it can become Gospel, when, and in so far as, it is rightly interpreted.' Again, J. Wirsching, *Was ist schriftgemäß*, uses the terminology of 'the Bible becoming scripture', and this is fundamental to his whole presentation. See especially his pp. 39–42, and cf. below, p. 177 n. I myself have not adopted his distinction, and 'scripture' and 'the Bible' are interchangeable throughout this book. I doubt whether the distinction would make sense to English readers (he says, p. 41, that 'there is a holy scripture, but no holy Bible'; but certainly 'the Holy Bible' is normal English usage, probably better established than 'holy scripture'); and I would think that the theological distinctions, which he expresses through this terminological opposition, could be otherwise stated. But for the present the only point to be made is his adherence to a basic pattern where the true effect of the Bible is seen only when something *becomes* something else.

culture and is not immanent within it, and it has to be studied with a method which is attuned for the hearing of this Word of God.

These ideas, expressed in Word-of-God terminology, seem at first sight to deal with many of the difficult problems posed by the Bible. They seem to assert its central importance, while avoiding the danger of bibliolatry. They accept its human and historical character, but do not find this to conflict with its function as mediator of revelation. They subordinate the Bible to the higher reality of God's self-revelation, but continue to maintain the essential place of scripture in all decisions about what is or is not revelation. They thus appear to express a middle way, which does justice to both sides of the reality.

In fact however the use of the term 'Word of God' does not seem to have solved the problems posed by the Bible in our time, and there has been a great decrease of interest in this term in recent years. For example, in the recent World Council of Churches discussion the phrase 'Word of God' scarcely occurs at all either in the preliminary study document or in the final report; and no attention is given to such schemes as the threefold form of the Word of God, or the double aspect of the Bible as Word of God and Word of Man. If one asks why these finely elaborated ideas have rather lost their effectiveness, the following can perhaps be suggested as an explanation:

(*a*) These ideas belonged too much to the world of systematic theology, of dogmatics, and had too little contact with the world of actual biblical scholarship. The exegetical scholar, working on the biblical texts in detail, was often at a loss to know where these ideas fitted in or what application they could have. This alienation from the world of scholarly exegesis was, in fact, one of the great weaknesses of the Barthian theology; it was unable to accept the contemporary exegete for what he was. The recent ecumenical discussion, by contrast, has had a strong exegetical emphasis and began, as already pointed out, from a study of exegetical practice.

(*b*) The interest in hermeneutics shifted the focus of the entire discussion. Its problem, if one can state it starkly, was not the difference between divine and human but the difference between ancient and modern. The question was: given that this was thought in biblical times, how is it to be re-stated in the modern situation, where the background and the problems are different? For this newer question the schemes built around the conception of the

Word of God seemed to have little relevance.

(*c*) Moreover, even from a purely theological point of view these schemes can be questioned. There is, for instance, no good reason why the relationship between God and man in the person of Christ should be supposed to hold good also for the relationship of divine and human in the Bible; even if one accepts in the fullest way a formula like the Chalcedonian about the person of Christ, there is no reason why it should be applicable also to the Bible (for which, needless to say, it was not designed).[4] Equally doubtful is the reasoning by which three so different entities as the person of Christ, the written scripture and the preaching of the church are arranged in a pattern as three 'forms of the Word of God'. One does not deny that this pattern *can* be made; but one does deny that it *must* be made. But if the pattern is not *mandatory*, one can perhaps suggest quite other patterns. The very elaborateness of these analogies, and the strictness with which they were followed up, makes them all the more useless once one loses the conviction of their applicability.

We may therefore sum up this section as follows: it is indeed stimulating to consider in what sense one may speak of the Bible as the Word of God, but we cannot now expect any decision on this question in itself to solve the uncertainties now existing about the status of the Bible. Nevertheless this survey has been valuable, because it shows the sort of range of meaning of which the term 'Word of God' is capable. Moreover, in spite of the deficiencies which have appeared in these ideas, we should not be blind to the important good effects which they have had in their time. There are doubtless many who have not yet reckoned with them and who may well find them profoundly liberating. If, as I suggest, theologies of the Barthian type were in their attitude to the Bible more conservative than appeared at first sight, and more remote from historical and critical exegesis, this is not only a negative judgment; for one of the great achievements of such theologies was to form a bridge by which people of very conservative tendencies could cross over into the main stream of Protestant Christianity.[5]

---

[4] I was myself already arguing along these lines in my review of J. K. S. Reid's *The Authority of Scripture* in *SJT* xi (1958), pp. 86–93, especially pp. 89f.

[5] It is significant that W. Hordern, in discussing the 'new conservatism' in America, asks the question 'Will this movement produce the real in-

3. Authority

'Authority' is the term which has been most widely used in recent studies of the status of the Bible. It is a relational or hierarchic concept; it tries to order and grade the various powers, or sources of ideas, that may influence us. The church, or the Christian, or the preacher, is thought of as being subject to a variety of forces which may act upon the mind. The notion of authority defines the priority of one such force over another. One may for instance subsume all valid influences under two headings, scripture and church tradition, and hold that these have equal authority – a traditional Roman Catholic position. One may give prime authority to scripture and maintain that tradition has rightful influence only when it is firmly graded as below the supreme authority of scripture – a traditional Protestant position. One may say that the influences bearing upon the church and the Christian are innumerable and unclassifiable, and that no definite ordering or assignment of priorities between them is possible – one of the more 'radical' positions being argued at the present day. In all such cases 'authority' is used in an attempt to relate or to grade the forces bearing upon Christian belief and action.

The conception of 'norm' is more or less the same thing. If we say that scripture is 'normative', it means that it is the final court of appeal, the highest of the tests, to which Christian thoughts and actions have to be subjected. There may be various grades of things having some sort of authority, but that which is normative has the highest and final authority.

'Authority' and 'norm' thus define relations. They define (i) the relation between the Bible and ourselves, so that the Bible may be seen as something binding upon us, something to which we have to submit ourselves; and (ii) the relation between the Bible and other documents or sources of knowledge which might also influence our minds or actions at the same time.

There are several advantages in the use of these terms:

(*a*) 'Authority', in comparison (say) with 'inspiration', removes the emphasis from the *origins* of the Bible; equally, it removes the emphasis from the question of accuracy, inerrancy, and infallibility. These points, though stressed by fundamentalists, are actually of

---

heritors of Barth's theology?' See his *New Directions in Theology Today*, Vol. I: *Introduction*, p. 95.

marginal theological importance. The major theological questions concern the balance of influence between scripture and church tradition, or between scripture and contemporary philosophical and cultural trends; and for handling these questions the concept of authority is well adapted.

(*b*) It can indeed be argued that, if there is to be authority, there must be a ground for this authority; and that this brings us back to the matter of origins, of inspiration, of accuracy and inerrancy. This argument however is not necessarily valid. It can be replied that these are really minor points; that on the origins and inspiration of the Bible our knowledge is defective; and that the decision about authority itself is the main theological decision. Moreover, it can be argued, and would generally be argued, that the real ground for the authority of the Bible does not lie within the nature of the Bible itself; rather, it lies beyond the Bible, in the authority of God himself.[6] Or, to set out more fully the kind of argument which would commonly be advanced, the Bible derives its authority not from its own character and nature, but from the events which it relates. These are the events upon which Christians depend and to which they owe their salvation. The Bible is the written work which has emerged from these events, and emerged from them through a faith in their saving quality on the part of the biblical writers. The Bible thus has authority, and should rightly govern our lives and thoughts, because it is thus related to the fundamental events of salvation. Its authority does not rest upon what it is in itself but upon the events of salvation, of which it is the written – and therefore the permanent and permanently available – expression.

(*c*) This view in turn is very liberating to those troubled by difficulties about the exact historical nature of the saving events; it permits their exact historical nature, and the relation between them and the biblical narratives, to be left somewhat vague. The Bible has emerged from these past events as an interpretation of

[6] But – since I shall not return to this formulation of the matter – does the phrase 'the authority of God' really mean anything? I would have thought that 'authority' has a useful function when used of that which is *under* God but *over* men; applied to God himself, it seems to me to be otiose, since if one believes in God at all the concept 'God' seems to imply (analytically) something like authority. Such authority may be 'necessary' but contributes nothing new. It is of human and historical quantities that the attribution or non-attribution of authority is significant.

them in faith; it does not offer an exact historical transcript of them, and may indeed be confused, contradictory or in error about the historical facts. The events nevertheless, whatever their historical character, are the centre of salvation; and the authority of the Bible derives from the saving content of these events and the faith that responded to it, and not from the accuracy of its historical reporting.

(*d*) Thus 'authority' can be used in application to the Bible without implying any perfection of the Bible, without idolizing or absolutizing it. It can be used to say that, granted the historical and time-conditioned nature of the Bible, the accidents of its formation and its imperfections in historical reporting, it nevertheless is acknowledged as an authority of first grade, or of such and such other grade, in the government of Christian thought and life. This flexibility of 'authority' is certainly the chief reason why it has become the principal term for use in discussions of the status of the Bible, especially since 'inspiration' has been so marked by suggestions of fundamentalism.

In spite of these advantages, the suitability of the term 'authority' has recently been running into difficulties also. In the World Council of Churches study considerable care was taken to discuss 'authority' in order to clarify what is meant and to avoid undesirable misunderstandings; and a certain body of opinion would have preferred to avoid the term 'authority' altogether.[7]

The present difficulties with the idea of authority would seem to include:

(*a*) There appears to be a general crisis of authority at the present time. It affects not only the Bible but also the authority of the church, of bishops, Popes and other church leaders, of constitutions, legal systems and governments, of teachers and professors, and last but not least of parents and the older generation, as members of it are painfully aware. The World Council of Churches preliminary study says:

There appears to be a general crisis of authority at the present time, or at least the notion of authority is different. Authority is

[7] See 'Four Preliminary Considerations on the Concept of Authority', by E. Jüngel, G. Krodel, R. Marlé and J. D. Zizioulas, in *Ecumenical Review* xxi (1969), pp. 150–66, also ibid., pp. 141f., and *Louvain 1971*, esp. pp. 13f.

no longer conceded *a priori*, but is accepted only where it actually proves itself as such. Accordingly, it becomes increasingly difficult to assert biblical authority in a general way.[8]

(*b*) This, if true, seems to mean several different things. First of all, it means that in the present situation the use of the term 'authority' will give a bad impression. The question is one, therefore, of either explaining one's intentions better, or else using a different term. The 'Preliminary Considerations' by Jüngel and others, referred to above, are in part attempts at the former; they display a concern to explain authority in such a way as to make the term less offensive and more flexible. Jüngel[9] makes a distinction between the authoritarian and the authoritative. The former applies to an authority which uses force or constraint, and does not make its claim so evident that people can freely accept it. 'Authoritative' on the other hand applies to an authority which makes the rightfulness of its demands so evident that people, while realizing the possibility of objections, will freely admit their rightfulness. Biblical authority, in these terms, should be authoritative and not authoritarian. There is however little chance that such fine distinctions could be sustained in ordinary usage.[10]

It is in fact ironical that 'authority' should be somewhat discredited, on the grounds of its supposedly hard and dictatorial connotations, when (as has been pointed out above) one main advantage of the term is its relative softness and flexibility in comparison with such older terms as 'inspiration'.

(*c*) It is conceivable that one should therefore look for another term. But if this simply means another word which has the same range as 'authority', very little is gained. The question must rather be, whether the organization of the whole subject under the concept of 'authority' should be continued, or whether an entirely different organization of the matter has to be considered. It is this question, rather than the mere search for another term, which motivates those who wish to speak not of 'authority' but of the *role*, the *influence*, or the *function* of scripture.[11]

(*d*) If the term 'authority' is so defined as to make it more flexible and to increase the emphasis on free decision and acceptance, this

[8] *Ecumenical Review*, ibid., p. 138.
[9] Ibid., pp. 150f.
[10] Rightly so *Louvain 1971*, p. 14.
[11] *Louvain 1971*, ibid.

may only create a confusion or produce something which the average person will not recognize as 'authority' at all. The final report of the World Council of Churches study (*Louvain 1971*), seeking just this flexibility, seems to me to be very confused in exactly this regard. Let us distinguish between a 'hard' and a 'soft' idea of authority. A 'hard' idea would mean that the authority of the Bible was (i) antecedent to its interpretation, and (ii) general in its application. The reader or user of the Bible would be expected to *expect* that biblical passages would be authoritative and therefore illuminating; this would be so whether it was one biblical passage or another, and this expectation would be firm *before* the interpretation was carried out, and not therefore be a decision based afterwards upon the results of the interpretation. A 'soft' idea of authority would suggest that authority was (i) posterior to interpretation and application and (ii) limited accordingly to the passages where an authoritative effect had in fact been found. The Louvain report seems to me to vary unaccountably between soft accounts of authority and hard ones.[12]

(*e*) One must, I submit, accept that the dominant strain in the authority concept is a legal one, and that as a legal one it has to be what I have called 'hard', i.e. antecedent and general; moreover, this is the way in which the idea of biblical authority has very generally been applied in much of our history, at least in the West. It should therefore not be surprising if the average person, hearing the word 'authority', understands it in the hard sense; or if he, discovering that it is really being used in the soft sense, feels that he is being tricked with double talk. Nor, in view of the legal background of the concept, should it be surprising if reservations about

---

[12] E.g., the account of 'authority' on pp. 13f. seems very 'soft'; the Bible 'makes the Word of God audible and is therefore able to lead men to faith . . . men are arrested by the message of the Bible . . . they hear God speaking to them from the Bible'. Again (p. 20), 'What we mean is rather that through the Bible God proves himself to be the Lord and the Redeemer.' All of this appears to be 'soft' argumentation; and a sign of its softness is the fact that what it says about the Bible would be true also of other things than the Bible. But in the concluding paragraphs of the report we seem to pass over to a 'hard' understanding, e.g. '2. At the same time, of course [*sic*], the Bible *must* [my italics] be read with the expectation that it can disclose the truth to us.' From it 'we are not free to select at will'. It is (3) 'a critical court of appeal to which the Church *must constantly* [my italics] defer'.

its application to the Bible come from the Eastern Orthodox side, as in Zizioulas's assertion: 'In the history of Christianity the problem of authority appears to be a "Western problem".'[13] These considerations, if valid, suggest that, if we are moving from a hard view of biblical authority to a soft one, this would best be expressed as a move away from the authority concept altogether.

One might indeed argue that, alongside the legal authority concept, our language does contain a more personal and more religious strain, best known from the New Testament with its 'He spoke with authority'. This type of authority, involving direct personal impressiveness and carrying of conviction, seems closer to what is intended in a soft construction of authority. The soft construction could thus religiously be the stronger. But the problem with this more personal view of authority is to apply it precisely to *the Bible*; for such authority can certainly be found elsewhere than in the Bible, while on the other hand it is not automatically clear that it is to be found throughout the Bible itself.

(*f*) It is a question whether the 'authority' concept is really indigenous to the Christian tradition. In the sense found in 'the authority of the Bible', it is not really a biblical term. When we read that Jesus spoke with authority, or similar phrases, that is a somewhat different sense from the 'authority' which a book like the Bible can have over those who base their decisions upon it. We may wonder whether 'authority' is not a product of Roman law and government, one which in due course came to be at home in the church, being applied particularly to the authority exercised by the ecclesiastical hierarchy; and whether its application to the Bible may be an extension from this history.

(*g*) The final, and in some ways the most serious, difficulty in the 'authority' concept is the following: it no longer fits the intellectual structure in which theological work is carried on. In the past, until fairly recent times, almost the whole of theology was an authority structure. Thinking was done within a framework where authority existed and authoritative sources were laid down and defined. Not only theology, but also other aspects of church life, were authority structures. Within this general framework of authority it was natural that the status of the Bible also should be defined in terms of authority.

All this has now altered. The setting of theology is now ecu-

[13] *Louvain 1971*, p. 14; *Ecumenical Review*, ibid., p. 166.

menical and its connection with denominational legal structures has disappeared, apart from minor survivals; there are no longer denominational theologies, and the means of enforcing them have faded out of existence. Theology is characteristically pluralistic and theologians, apart from those who sigh nostalgically for old times, accept this fact, not just as a fact but as a good thing. Within the older authority structures the authority of the Bible occupied a high place in the hierarchy: theoretically at least it was one of the very highest courts of appeal for all sorts of authority, and it therefore had a defined place, very high in the hierarchical order. It was scarcely doubted that the appeal to scripture formed a major ground for discriminating between theologies, for preferring one and rejecting another. This is no longer in effect the case. The grounds for discriminating between one theology and another are multifarious but can certainly not be reduced to an ultimate appeal to scripture. Rather than scripture standing as an agreed authority, ready for use as criterion for any theology, each theology contains within itself (or may do so) an account of its own relation to the Bible. Within this newer context the idea of the 'authority' of the Bible has become anachronistic.

(*h*) To return to our 'soft' view of authority, it might be argued that the real authority is built upon *cumulative experience*. When we have read a biblical passage, we have found that it has 'spoken to us with authority' (in the more personal and religious sense, see [*e*] above); and this has happened so often that we become convinced it will always happen, and will happen also elsewhere in the Bible. Certainly this argument correctly reproduces the mental and biographical process by which many people become convinced of the authority of the Bible. When carried beyond this, however, and given the *logical* status of the *ground* for belief in biblical authority, it is manifestly wrong. Many of those who take part in the modern discussion have indeed found that some biblical passages do thus 'speak with authority' but that this cannot be generalized into a universal rule: even passages which 'speak with authority' to some may fail to do so to others, and the experience based upon some passages can certainly not be extended to all others.

To many of these points we shall have to return at some later stage. They are sufficient to indicate that the concept of 'authority', in spite of the advantages which it has, can by no means be taken as a certainly adequate organizing bracket for the discussion of the place of the Bible in Christian faith and life. We therefore pass to another possible way of organizing the discussion, namely under various *functions* exercised by the Bible.

4. Function

We turn therefore to ask if it is possible to concentrate not on the authority of the Bible but on an analysis of the functions which it exercises. What difference would this make? Possible advantages would seem to include:

(*a*) The problem of the Bible within Christianity appears to split up into separate questions, each of them requiring independent answers, according to the different functions which the Bible exercises. One might, for example, distinguish such separate questions as:

(i) How is the Bible used in deciding between different theological possibilities?

(ii) Can theology be pursued also on a more or less non-biblical (e.g. on a philosophical) basis?

(iii) How far is the preacher bound to base his talk upon biblical exposition?

(iv) Can the church use the Bible in addressing the non-Christian world, as well as in informing the churchgoer?

(v) Can the Bible offer ethical guidance on matters of the present day?

It is possible to argue that the relation between the Bible and the problem posed differs in each case, and that therefore a general picture of biblical authority will be distorted for each case; or at least that it will have to be amplified for the special circumstances of each.

(*b*) This is perhaps to put the same point in another way: The problem of the Bible seems to have become above all a problem of *processes*, the processes by which one interprets the biblical text and the processes by which one relates it to the questions of today. This insight agrees with the fact that the present questioning of the place of the Bible follows closely upon the discussion of interpretation, both in the World Council of Churches studies and in the general public of the churches. If in fact the interpretative processes are so decisive in their effect upon the meaning attributed to the text, then the centre of the question lies in these processes and not in an 'authority' of the Bible which would be either something antecedent to these processes (the 'hard' view of authority) or something recognized after they had been completed (the 'soft' view).[14] These processes can be restated as the functions of various persons in their work with the Bible – the function of the historical scholar,[15] the biblical theologian, the systematic theologian, the preacher, the apologist and so on.[16]

This differentiation of functions has become one of the dominating features of the modern theological scene. In theology, as in other fields of knowledge, the complexity of knowledge and the specialization of techniques has meant an increasing division of labour. This diversity of functions has been the cause of great tension and sometimes animosity in modern theology, taken as a whole. The various functions are not irreconcilable: historical scholarship, biblical exegesis, linguistic competence, and theology are not watertight compartments, within only one of which any person can belong. Indeed, the serious Christian has to make some attempt at more than one of them. But *mastery* within all of them is now impossible for any individual, and even for the most gifted a mastery of more than one is exceptional; even a field like Old Testament or New Testament is becoming too large for most of us. The matter has a purely professional side; but also it is a problem for the unity of theology, and thus for the unity of the comprehension of the Christian faith. It is now increasingly a problem of understand-

[14] Some older views of the matter suggested that the 'authority' of the Bible was the paramount concern and that interpretation would take care of itself as long as authority was secure; this belongs together with the idea that all error in interpretation comes from the intrusion of philosophies and non-biblical ideas, and that strict exclusion of these guarantees freedom for the sense of the Bible. The World Council study rightly recognizes that this view existed but must now be abandoned: 'We no longer suppose that the acceptance of biblical authority is a sure way to rightness in our exegesis, or even that its acceptance is a necessary precondition of right interpretation.' *Ecumenical Review*, ibid., p. 138, para. (v).

[15] One of the problems of an approach through authority is that it tends to exclude or ignore the work of the historical-critical scholar, in whose work the authority concept does not have a place.

[16] *Louvain 1971* gives the impression of supposing that the important thing is the move from a static (p. 213) concept to a relational concept (p. 14). This is a confusion. Authority is (at least in my terminology) a relational concept whether it is static or not, whether aggressive or accepted in freedom. It was thus always relational, even in the most conservative ideas. The move to processes and functions is a much more real difference.

ing – understanding the processes of thought and interpretation as they function in the work of those whose expertise is strange to us, and giving place to this functioning within our understanding of the total unity of theology. This diversity of functions will be in our mind as we look at the Bible from a number of different angles in the course of this book.

(c) One of the recurrent problems in all biblical interpretation is that of the apparent differences in value or in impact of different portions of the Bible. It has proved difficult to deal with this within the framework of an authority concept: to say that certain parts have less authority than others seems inevitably to downgrade them. It seems much more flexible to consider this question through the differentiation of functions. Thus it might be possible to say that within Christianity both Old and New Testaments had authority, but that their functions were different; or, again, that the function of the Wisdom Literature was different from that of the Prophetic, or the function of the Epistles different from that of the Gospels.

(d) As we saw in an earlier section, the term 'inspiration' has widely gone out of use because of the impasse in discussions with fundamentalism; 'authority' was adopted in part because of its greater flexibility in the same problems. But the possibility has to be considered that 'authority' has now come into the same impasse as 'inspiration'. While satisfying to the people in the centre of mainstream Christianity, dealing with the main theologies and the main trends of biblical study, it has ceased to be flexible and creative in the discussion with fundamentalism. A discussion of the functions of the Bible, or the processes through which it impinges upon Christian belief and action, might on the other hand offer a new way forward.

These then are some advantages which might accrue from the discussion of the Bible under the heading of its functions rather than its authority. What are the possible disadvantages of such a course?

(a) First, it may be felt that this proposal implies a purely descriptive approach, which will state the way in which the Bible functions as a matter of fact in present-day Christianity but makes no attempt to decide what *should* be done, what is right as against what is now happening. In other words, 'function' would suggest a neutral and phenomenological approach, perhaps something of a sociological description, while 'authority' would suggest claims, existential demands, and ethical imperatives.

In this there are two questions: first of all, is a treatment under function really a neutral and purely descriptive approach? Secondly, even if it is so, is a neutral and purely descriptive approach a bad thing in a case like this?

To take the second question first, all questions about biblical authority have for so long been moral, existential and emotionally loaded questions, that there is very good reason why an emotionally neutral approach should be taken. No one who knows Christian theology, and especially the more conservative and more biblical elements within it, can have doubts about the strong moral pressure and the heavy emotional loading of all questions such as 'Do you not accept the biblical teaching?' or 'Is that really a biblical idea?' or 'How can you square that with the words of St Paul in so-and-so?' Such emotional loading is nearly always in favour of the more conservative, or the more biblical, position. Since some centuries of this hectic pressurizing have still produced only limited agreement, there might be much sense in trying a different way.

But this argument is not entirely necessary to the case, for what is being proposed is not a neutral description of the way the Bible in fact functions. It would rather be a theologically critical account of the functions which it exercises, including both encouragement and criticism where appropriate.

(*b*) It might be argued that an approach through function would miss the essential point. The real problem, it would be said, is the decision in principle about the criterion for doctrine and ethics. An approach through varied functions might be a sophisticated way of evading this issue.

(*c*) Finally, it might be argued that the approach through functions was not really different from that through authority, that the word was different but the questions and answers in substance the same.

I do not propose to try and answer these questions at this point. The purpose of this chapter has been to open up the possibilities, to show that a variety of concepts exists under which the status of the Bible within Christian faith can be formulated. If this had not been done, there would have been a danger that the traditional formulations such as that in terms of authority would have been accepted as natural and inevitable without further discussion. I hope to have shown that the different formulations for the status of the Bible have different capacities, and that it is not a matter of course that we should adopt one of them rather than another. Having done this, I hope to leave it to the progress of our discussion to demonstrate which of the various possibilities (or which combination of several among them) may prove to be most convenient and appropriate.

III

CULTURAL RELATIVISM AND THE NEW RADICALISM

I have already said that in recent years very radical questions are being asked afresh about the centrality and the decisive importance which were traditionally ascribed to the Bible and which seemed to be reasserted with some success in the post-war biblical revival. This radical questioning is at least in part the occasion for the writing of this book; and it seems good that more should be said about it at this point.

As I have indicated, we cannot speak of any unified or clearly formulated position, which could easily be identified. My description of it rests upon the impression gained from many separate discussions; and one may quite possibly be unfair if one tries to classify together as one group all those who in these discussions have queried the centrality traditionally attached to the Bible. According to my own experience, however, certain common features do appear to emerge, and some of these will be delineated here. I do not mean the term 'radicalism' to be taken very seriously; all I mean is that the opinions being described are radical in their questioning of some traditional or accepted views of the status of the Bible. Whether they are radical in other respects lies beyond our enquiry. My presentation may well be too much coloured by my personal experience, but this seems to be inevitable because the subject itself is ill-defined.

As has already been said, the radical questioner of the status of the Bible is not ignorant of the arguments which in the post-war decades have raised that status to so high a point. He knows these arguments, but they do not convince him. The more he hears them, the more he doubts their cogency. A previous generation, perhaps, grew up in an atmosphere where biblical authority was much in dispute, and felt it an achievement when something of a settlement was reached; the younger generation, perhaps, growing up and educated in a situation where the status of the Bible was more highly valued, is less disposed to continue in this settled state. Or perhaps its members have been influenced by that stratum of opinion which never accepted the wide post-war consensus over biblical authority, which was pushed on to the defensive, but which now once again feels able to assert itself.

The newer radical opinion does not have to say that all the arguments, which were used to establish biblical authority at a high level, were *wrong*. In themselves they were, perhaps, quite justified chains of reasoning: the distinctiveness of Old Testament thought as against its environment, the distinctiveness likewise of the New Testament as against Hellenism, the history-based character of revelation, the once-and-for-all character of salvation and its relation to the 'apostolic' witnesses. All this might be justified, but it did not demonstrate that which was supposed to be demonstrated by it, namely the status of the Bible, this group of books and no other, as the supreme norm, criterion or authority to which Christians had to refer in their modern problems. Between the arguments that were offered and the results that were reached there existed a considerable gap; and this gap, radical opinion feels, had been filled in by a presupposition, not to say a sheer prejudice, in favour of the idea that the church should accept the Bible as the prime authority over its affairs. Against all such argument radical opinion returns the question: *Why the Bible?* Why should a group of ancient books have this dominant status? If a group of ancient books, then why *this* group of ancient books? And why in any case should anyone suppose that any objective external authority, in the shape of a group of books or any other shape at all, exists at all?

We have already noted incidentally one of the main features of this movement of thought, namely its emphasis on the modern situation. The weight of decision lies *now*, and not in what was thought two thousand years ago or more. What was thought long ago may indeed influence us in our decisions of today; but that is indeed the right proportion of the matter: it is we in our decision-making who may well take into account the Bible (but also other things as well); it is never the case that the Bible can make our decisions for us. As I wrote recently,

> The locus of the authority question has shifted. The critical question is no longer 'What was said back then?' but 'What should we say now?' The centre of the authority crisis . . . lies in the present day . . . The sense of doubt . . . arises from a concentration on that which is closer to the present-day decision as against that which is more remote.[1]

This dominance of the modern situation agrees well, of course, with the whole emphasis on relevance which has lately been popular, especially in certain currents of student opinion. But how does the church address itself to the modern world? Is the modern Christian isolated in his modernity, face to face alone with the modern world? To this it would seem that there are two possible answers. The first is more Bultmannian, more existentialist and more Protestant. The Christian is indeed alone with the modern world, and just there he has to take the existential decisions which grasp real existence. Naturally he has to be properly informed in every possible way. But there is no external authority which can decide for him; and indeed any attempt to let an external authority do this for him must only invalidate his decision by making it inauthentic. If the Bible (or, as would be more usually said, the gospel) came into this, it would not be, if I understand the position properly, to dictate the content of the decision, but rather to present in the most compelling form a claim that such a decision must be made. This would be one possibility.

The second possibility would be more communal, more historical and (in my experience) more Anglican. The essential context of the Christian in the modern world is his context within the church. It is the church that has to speak to the modern situation; and the church provides the Christian with a continuum of experience, extended through the contemporary world and extended historically into the past. That historical experience goes back to biblical times and can be drawn upon for contemporary decisions. But there is absolutely no reason why the *earliest* stage of that experience, i.e. the biblical stage, should be the primary one to be drawn upon, or why, if the earliest stage is to be drawn upon, it must be done purely through reference to the written documents of that period, i.e. the Bible. More recent stages of the church's

[1] *Interpretation* xxv (1971), pp. 36f.

experience are at least equally likely to be relevant, or are more likely to be so; and in any case the church, in making up its mind about present-day matters, will consider not only the Bible, and not only the totality of its own past experience, but also all sorts of other knowledge which comes to bear upon it from modern sciences which have comparatively little footing in the old tradition of the church.

If it is accepted that these two possibilities exist, it is the latter which will figure more prominently in this book, because it has figured more prominently in my experience, is in my opinion intrinsically more interesting, and has played a greater part in stimulating the recent ecumenical discussion of the whole matter. Some of the things which I shall say will apply also, however, to the former possibility.

Another tendency which is likely to accompany these views is an opposition against the *defining* and *ordering* of authorities. There are at any time many influences which bear upon the mind of the church as it makes a decision, and it is either wrong or impossible, or both, to classify and order these influences as a hierarchy of 'authorities'. To put it in another way, this tendency is one of opposition against the idea of a 'systematic' theology, the function of which would be the fixing of these relations. Thus, even if on some particular occasion the church had found that the guidance of scripture had been both preponderant and wholesome, it would not be able to generalize this as a principle or to forecast that at the next moment of difficulty, or at any future such moment, scripture would have this dominant role. This point of view is a distinct departure from the older theological tradition, which would seem to have striven for the clear statement of the authorities under which any theology set itself and which acted therefore as criterion of its validity. When the church makes up its mind, the criterion is simply: its own mind. It never was and never can be anything else. 'Whatever may be said in theory, I do not believe the Church ever does, or ever can, settle its questions by reference to some allegedly external and objective norm.'[2]

The third strand within this type of thinking, if I analyse it rightly, is a position which we may characterize as 'cultural relativism'. Since this position is important, and since it has not had wide discussion in previous works on the status of the Bible, it

[2] D. E. Nineham, *BJRL* lii (1969), 198f.

will require a more extended exposition:

The Bible, like all other literary works, is dependent on the cultural milieu (in fact, a plurality of cultural milieus) in which it was written. Our modern culture is different, and it is not possible that the same work, the Bible, can have the same meaning as it had in its own cultural milieu. Any work or text composed in an ancient time and an ancient culture has its meaning in that time and that culture, and in our time or culture may have a different meaning, or indeed may have no meaning at all.

If I understand the argument rightly, it goes on with this further point: this applies not only to the relation between our understanding and the text of the Bible, but also to the relation between the text of the Bible and the events related in it or observed by the writers. If there were events lying behind the biblical data, and if these events were interpreted in the Bible in a certain way, this was because the men of the Bible held cultural assumptions which made it meaningful to them to interpret in this way. Our culture is different and therefore the interpretations we give to events will necessarily be different from those given by the biblical writers.

> We are still bound in integrity to ask whether if we, with our twentieth-century background, had been there, we should have felt the historical events in question to demand any explanation in supernatural terms; and we can be sure that if so, the terms we should have used would not have been the ones used by the biblical writers.[3]

Objectors will be quick to argue that this point of view absolutizes our modern culture and judges others inferior by comparison with it. This objection has already, however, been seen and turned aside. Our culture is factually different and therefore the interpretations we give to events will necessarily be different from those given by the biblical writers. The question whether our interpretation is a *better* one simply does not arise; what is clear is that it cannot be the *same* one.

The biblical writers were themselves conditioned by the assumptions general in their own culture: for instance, by the sense of death as an enemy, or by the idea of a chaos which threatens to engulf the world, or by the notion of man as a body-soul entity. It was then normal, or at least generally thinkable, that one should be

[3] Nineham, *BJRL*, op. cit., p. 188.

troubled by the sense of sin and the fear of death, that one should long for immortality. We today do not generally think in this way; we do not fear death, or at least fear of it does not trouble our normal daily motivation in times of health and safety; we do not care about life after death and do not want to have immortality; we may have opinions about body-soul relations in man, but these do not derive from our religious belief; and we may find that we do not have any considerable sense of sin. Since the biblical assumptions are quite different, our perception of and interpretation of events must also be different from theirs.

Such differences exist not only between biblical times and our own, but also within the total biblical period, for the development of the Bible spans many centuries and wide diversities of culture. Some of the points just mentioned exemplify the deep oppositions within the Bible. Soul and body relationships are seen in quite a different way in early Old Testament times and in New Testament times. In much of the Old Testament death under good circumstances, i.e. in old age and in the midst of one's land and children, is a good, right and satisfying thing; it is not in any sense an 'enemy', and the metaphysical fear and horror of death is quite absent. On the question whether death is the end of a man's existence, or whether there is a future for him after death, different cultures within the Bible answer differently; and thus it is only in one segment of the Bible that problems of resurrection and immortality are meaningful. The rising of Jesus from the dead, had it occurred in the eighth century BC, would have meant something different or would have been totally meaningless. All interpretations of events, and thus all theologies, are culturally conditioned in this respect.

Thus, if we adopt cultural relativism in an extreme form, it would seem that there is no sense in which the Bible can be 'authoritative' for us. The effort, the striving, to adapt biblical thought for our society is in vain, for in fact nothing along this line can be accomplished. Far from the Bible being normative or mandatory for the thinking of the modern Christian, we begin to appreciate the Bible as it is only when we realize that it can never be either of these things in any exclusive sense.

According to this school of thought, the idea of biblical authority is logically dependent on another idea: the idea that human nature in essence remains unchanged through time and through the vicissitudes of cultural change. This we now know to be untrue. There is no universal human nature, only man as he is in each out of a great variety of quite different cultures. A work like the Bible, which is the product of one particular cultural situation (or more correctly, which is a compilation of works, the products of a group of such situations over a long period of change) cannot therefore be authoritative in any decisive sense for other cultures; the idea is so absurd as not to be worth discussing.

It will be illuminating at this point to compare the position of cultural relativism with the position reached in the hermeneutic discussion with Bultmann at its centre.[4] There are clear common elements, for example the strong sense of historical difference and the interest in the possibility of interpreting, and making relevant, to modern man the materials of an ancient tradition. Bultmann also is regarded by many as something of a sceptic, and some may think of him as partially responsible for present questionings of the status of the Bible. But the stress laid upon right interpretation by Bultmann, and the whole programme of demythologization, appear to depend on a strong conviction that the Bible is the source from which the message must come. Conversely, interpretation is necessary and, given the right procedure, possible. For modern man the biblical message is locked up by reason of its mythical clothing; but an interpretation which will remove this mythical element and set free the true message is thus essential, and what is thus set free will indeed be the authoritative content for Christian faith and preaching today. In this sense Bultmann seems to belong to a rather *traditional* Protestant position about biblical authority.[5] By contrast, scholars holding the 'cultural relativism' position might say that, no matter how good our interpretative technique, the use of it would not decide our questions of today, since the Bible, even if rightly interpreted, is only one factor among many in the making of decisions. The questioning of the status of the Bible is in fact much more radical than anything that was revealed in the discussion about hermeneutics; and indeed the hermeneutics discussion seems now to

---

[4] Cf. also below, pp. 49f.
[5] I have published in *Interpretation* xxv (1971), pp. 30ff., a somewhat analogous argument about Bultmann's view of the Old Testament. Bultmann is often regarded as very negative towards the Old Testament; but there are also elements in his thought which suggest that its authority is indispensable.

have had a rather biblicistic basis throughout, the whole question being 'What is the right way of interpreting the Bible for today?'

Finally, the school of thought which we are describing is very sensitive to the apparent *absurdities* involved in ideas of biblical authority. The idea that the Bible, of all things, can serve as the dominant criterion for Christian faith and ethics in its modern situation is a towering irrationality. What else can one say of a situation where scholars meticulously search through St Paul's writings in order to decide whether women can come to church without hats? One might wave the example aside with a tolerant air, on the ground that all Christendom has suddenly agreed to ignore the women's hat question; but the point is that this sort of thing is just what happens when the Bible is taken to be decisive for present-day problems. To search painfully through Thessalonians, in order to discover whether God still has or has not a separate purpose for the Jewish people, is just the same kind of fantasy. Would it not be better to admit that Paul's judgments about the Jews in the Thessalonian letters were just a result of bad temper, 'an outburst of exasperation'?[6] If one had come back to him a few weeks later, would he not have admitted that what he had written did not do justice to his own mind, much less to the mind of Christ? And if, at the most, by some stretch of the imagination one can see that these Pauline passages were right for their own time, should we not admit that when applied to our modern situation they are simply a lot of nonsense?

And let us not confine this to instances which may be marginal, for the principle is the same even in matters which the biblical writers regarded as having prime theological importance: let us admit that even there we may have to regard their views as distorted, one-sided, inadequate, or *just plain wrong*. After all, does

---

[6] W. Neil, quoted in D. E. Nineham, *BJRL*, ibid., p. 182, as expressing the view of 'many English commentators'. There is indeed an obvious reply, namely that psychological explanation is one thing and theological validity another; Plato may have written the *Republic* in a fit of bad temper, but its philosophical validity is another matter. But this obvious objection does not entirely deal with Dr Nineham's argument: he is saying, I think, that *theologically* Paul's assertions make no sense, and that therefore the psychological explanation is the best and most charitable. So long as we suppose that his assertions *must somehow* make theological sense, we are prevented from adopting this better explanation. If in the *Republic* we find something which is philosophical nonsense, we may consider that Plato had a touch of indigestion at that point.

not modern biblical study show us how often the biblical writer was inspired not by a zeal for the pure truth or for accurate theological statement but by polemics against other biblical writers, the emphasis or tendency (and even tendentiousness) of whose works he wants to correct? Has not the detection of this conflict of tendency between different biblical writers become one of the main tools of the biblical scholar?

Basically, therefore, it is alleged, once it is supposed that the Bible has some kind of supreme normative or authoritative function, there falls upon the interpreter the absurd and quite unnecessary burden of somehow showing that the Bible in the end of the day is *right*. This leads exegetes into all sorts of contortions which would be quite unnecessary if, let us say, the opinions of St Paul were agreed to be no more than just that, the opinions of St Paul. In the heyday of the revival of biblical authority, it was apparently supposed that the authority of the Bible was in fact the key to its right interpretation, that if one accepted it as authoritative this fact would guide one to the right exegesis.[7] Quite the contrary is the case. Only when we give up the futile expectation that the Bible's utterances will express what is right and authoritative can we begin to face it for what it really is, something belonging to an environment entirely different from our own, in which the questions and answers also were entirely different.

Similarly, those who follow this same approach to the Bible are impressed by the *accidental* nature of the process which led to the formation of the Bible as we know it. The acceptance of books as canonical did not proceed on the basis of theological considerations which we could share today, but on the basis partly of geography and the rivalries of the major churches in ancient times, partly of historical accident, partly of sheer fantasies or falsehoods, through which books were attributed to 'apostles'. Moreover, the question is not directed only at the choice of the books which came to be included in the canon of holy scripture; it is also a question of the idea that there should be any holy scripture at all. The reduction of the oldest traditions to writing may have been a mistake or worse; the production of the first gospel may have been 'the first serious failure of nerve on the part of the infant church' (R. H. Lightfoot, reported by Nineham[8]); more seriously still, the production of a holy scripture may be considered as the clearest demonstration of

[7] *Ecumenical Review* xxi (1969), p. 138, para. (v); see above, p. 31 n.
[8] Nineham, *BJRL*, ibid., p. 198.

the presence of original sin in the early Church.[9]

With this limited outline we do no more than introduce to readers the problems of the Bible as seen from one point of view. We shall at a later stage have to return to say more about this viewpoint, but some kind of preliminary assessment may well be useful here. In general, I would say this: I am not convinced by the arguments which I have described, and do not agree with the main part of them; but I do think that they have brought us to a new stage of the discussion, which is likely to be stimulating and fruitful, and it has to be admitted that some elements in them are justified in part. Finally, though I am not convinced by these arguments, I do not feel that I have fully adequate counter-arguments to advance against them.

The strengths of this sort of radical position, and its weaknesses, seem to be as follows:

The view that the church has to say what it believes today, and not merely address people on the basis of what was believed by biblical writers some thousands of years ago, seems in itself entirely justified. On one side this is a matter of integrity and honesty; people rightly expect us to say *what we believe*, and to be ready to take responsibility for that as our belief. Moreover, as a matter of practical procedure it is probable that the church, in speaking to the general public, tries in fact to express its own present belief in present-day language; in other words, it refrains from addressing the general public, and especially the sceptics within it, through the form of lengthy exegeses of Genesis or of St Paul. This follows from the fact that, whatever the degree of authority attached to the Bible within the church, no such authority can be presumed to attach to it in the minds of the non-believing public. It is only within the conservative evangelical approach that the churches still try to approach the outsider with the authority of holy scripture set in the front line of demands. The more generally accepted priority has been the opposite: far from taking the Bible as a basis and proceeding from it towards the birth of personal faith, it is felt that the position of the Bible is so problematic and delicate that its difficulties can be approached only after personal faith in Christ is already present. Thus the demand that the church should speak by articulating what it itself today believes is not so unusual a sugges-

[9] Cf. C. F. Evans, *Is 'Holy Scripture' Christian?*, pp. 6f., and below, p. 128.

tion and probably fits in with what is already accepted by many, including many who are quite conservative about biblical authority.

All this however only moves the question one stage back. The question now is not 'How does the church express its mind to the modern world?' but 'How does the church make up its own mind in the first place?' Here all the questions present themselves once again; for it will be said that the church, however it eventually expresses itself to the modern world, both should accept and does in fact accept the predominant guidance of the Bible in its work of educating itself, informing itself, building itself up (to paraphrase the old word 'edify'), sifting and discriminating between all the opinions which are alleged to represent Christian faith, and meeting the challenges which come to it from the surrounding environment.

This question we shall for the present leave open. It would be impossible to say how the church makes up her mind without first taking into account all the considerations which are to be unfolded in the course of this book, plus no doubt others which will not be mentioned here. We simply accept the claim that the church in speaking to the modern world has to say what it today believes; this is at least partly, if not entirely, legitimate. But it does not make so much difference to the authority or function of the Bible as would at first seem to be the case, since the locus of function of the Bible would then only be moved to another point, namely to the making up of the modern church's mind. The argument would thus serve only to put in question any *purely biblical* manner of speech on the part of the modern world, any attempt simply to reproduce the Bible without any element of weighing, balancing, interpretation, criticism and translation into modern idiom by the modern church. In questioning such a procedure as that, the argument is certainly justified; but it is also exaggerated, since such a procedure has not been envisaged or intended by those who have regarded the Bible as authoritative or normative. The matter does however raise the issue how far the Bible can serve purely as a reserve criterion, behind the scenes in the formation of the church's mind, and how far the church also uses the Bible as the overt instrument of its communication. This we shall leave to a later point.

We can now continue with a preliminary discussion of some of the issues raised by cultural relativism.

(*a*) Cultural relativism, at least in the form in which I have stated it, appears to encapsulate man within his own contemporary culture and leave him with no bridge by which he can communicate with any other culture. Now there is no reason to deny or minimize the substantial difficulties of transcultural communication. But, we may urge, cultures – or at least cultures like that of biblical times and that of our own – are not homogeneous monads but are mixtures, which include internal conflicts and which have connections with other cultures, separated linguistically, geographically and temporally. These conflicts and these connections provide at any one time a variety of possibilities and options. Cultures are not mutually exclusive and mutually incomprehensible entities. A certain degree of cultural mixing is possible; it is in fact, in the cultures with which we are here concerned, normal; and, finally, it is salutary.

(*b*) Thus the argument which we are discussing appears to define too narrowly what is 'a culture', to confine it within too thin a temporal band. Where a culture has a memory of its past, then that remembered past would appear to be a part of that culture; and the power of that past is the greater where it is made available through literary preservation and through the attribution of high value, whether literary or religious, to this heritage. Modern Christianity or modern Judaism are sub-cultures in which a particular remembered past is part of the modern culture. This past has to be continually assimilated, for instance by the young, and by those entering for the first time the Christian community; it has indeed to be re-assimilated again and again by those who are within it. Assimilation of this past culture is in fact a normal feature of the activity of the modern religious culture, at least in typical mainstream Christianity. This cultural transmission is a one-way process: we concern ourselves with the understanding of our cultural past, but the converse is not true, that the men of the Bible could have assimilated our more modern reflections and developments. It is because it is a past-future relation of this kind that communicability between biblical and modern times is not only possible but natural; it is thus a quite different case from the problems of culture contact where two groups come together who have had no previous common basis whatever.

(*c*) Cultural relativism in the form discussed appears to be associated with, or to lead to, a marked passivity of Christian faith and theology in relation to whatever happens to pass current in the culture of our own time. If the position is true, we cannot understand things otherwise than as is made possible by patterns present in our contemporary culture. Quite apart from the criticism that this position would be unworthy of Christian faith, even in sociological terms this seems unlikely. Even taking Christianity in the fullest sense as part of the contemporary culture, one would expect it to make its own input into the culture of the time and not only to receive the output of the remainder of the culture.

I do not put this forward as a criticism of the personal position of friends who espouse the cultural relativist position; for they, in my experience, are commonly people of some considerable independence of mind, of radicalism and nonconformity – a fact which both does them credit as persons and does damage to the force of their own argument.

(*d*) What of the question whether human nature remains permanently the same? It would be foolishness for this author even to embark on the solving of such a conundrum, and only some remarks will be offered here. Unquestionably the common Christian viewpoint in this matter is that human nature does not alter; one would hardly say that this is *doctrine*, with any real theological authorization; but it is the sort of thing that is continually said by preachers and others when they use the Bible. Perhaps we might agree that, whether human nature changes or does not, human situations do change, and the problems and difficulties of one age are not those of another. When the modern church-goer is solemnly assured that he is in essentially the same situation as the Prophet Moses, or Nicodemus, or Cornelius, he ought to burst out laughing.

So far as I know, the question here involved has never been well identified or analysed. The typical procedure in these matters would seem to rest on an idea of analogy. Granted that there are changes in the human situation, there exists – it is supposed – sufficient analogy between a biblical situation and a modern to make it possible to apply the former to the latter. But how great does the similarity have to be, and how great a degree of difference can be tolerated?

The best illustration of this, to my mind, is the depiction of the Pharisees and Sadducees in the Gospels, or the corresponding picture of the Judaizing Christian implied by St Paul in his doctrine of justification by faith (as against justification by works of the law). I do not here ask how far these depictions and arguments are fair to the historical realities of the Pharisees, Sadducees, Jewish Christians and others involved; that is also a significant question, but not the one that concerns us now. I ask how close is the relation between these persons and ideas as depicted in the New Testament and the positions and ideas of people in the twentieth century. What is the proportion of similarity and of difference? Would it be wild to say 40% of similarity, 60% of difference?[10] Yet this is a stronger case than many, and theologically it is a very important instance: Reformation teaching discerned a very strong analogy between Judaism, or Judaizing Christianity, on the one hand and late mediaeval Roman Catholicism on the other; and this insight lies at the roots of Protestantism. This analogy continues to work in the mind of every evangelical clergyman who discerns in his people a struggle between a trust in 'good works' and a 'saving faith'. There are of course differences: his parishioners, for instance, are not in the slightest inclined to have themselves circumcised or to keep the Mosaic law; but he pushes these differences aside as irrelevant. By contrast, a thorough-going cultural relativism would rate the differences so high as to leave no significant similarity at all.

Is there then a constant reality which we call 'human nature', or is it so culturally diversified that no constant elements remain? We must be grateful to cultural relativism for putting the question in so sharp a form. I do not feel able to offer any proper answer at the present stage; some further considerations should perhaps be taken into account first of all:

(i) Clearly, the question of cultural relativism has a philosophical aspect. Herein however lies one of the paradoxes of the present radical questioning of the status of the Bible. It is at least possible to suppose that this radical questioning, as we now find it in the English-speaking world, has some association with the influence of empiricist philosophies.[11] Cultural relativism as we have described it seems, however, to belong to an idealist, and not an

---

[10] K. Stendahl, 'Biblical Theology', *IDB* I, p. 420: 'This ingenious translation or application of Pauline theology may be 80 per cent correct but left 20 per cent of Paul inexplicable – and consequently distorted in a certain sense the true picture of Pauline thought.' See also his famous article 'The Apostle Paul and the Introspective Conscience of the West', *Harvard Theological Review* lvi (1963), pp. 199–215.

[11] Cf. above, p. 9.

empiricist, point of view. It lays emphasis not on entities objectively existing in the external world, not on modes of verification, and not on a common world existing antecedently to our perception of it; rather it emphasizes the human consciousness and the peculiar culturally conditioned forms of it, which forms in turn determine the way in which we may represent to ourselves the world. In this sense it seems far from clear that the cultural relativist position fits in with an empiricist point of view; and, so far as I know, it would not necessarily find wide acceptance among English philosophers.

(ii) Further, it is interesting to make a comparison with the 'biblical theology' of recent years. One feature of this movement was its tendency to absolutize the Hebraic culture of the Bible. On the one hand it separated it with excessive severity from other contiguous and comparable cultures, and on the other it dumped the whole thing, the Hebrew 'way of thinking', upon the modern Christian consciousness as an authoritative load of cultural baggage which simply had to be carried.[12] All this was part of an impulse to assert biblical authority and the centrality of the Old Testament. Our present cultural relativism goes in the opposite direction: it reduces the emphasis on the Bible and places the Old Testament in a more marginal position. But the general ideas about human culture, ideas of the acute separation of each culture and the deep difficulty of communication between them, seem to be alike. Cultural relativism in theology stands in complete opposition to the previous 'biblical theology' stage; but even in that opposition it has taken over something of the isolated-culture position of the other. In its contradiction of that earlier position it has also accepted something of its heritage. This fact, if true, seems to constitute something of a weakness.

(iii) Moreover a certain amount of the comparison with Bultmann may be recapitulated here.[13] Bultmann also makes a deep contrast between cultures: the culture of biblical man is mythological throughout, while that of modern man is more scientific in character and lacks this mythological element. There is therefore a

---

[12] Cf. Stendahl, *IDB* I, p. 427b; similarly, Barr, *Old and New in Interpretation*, pp. 58f. For opposition to the necessity of accepting 'Hebrew thought' in modern Christianity, cf. Nineham, *Authority*, p. 94; cf. below, pp. 86f.

[13] Cf. above, pp. 41f.

communication problem between the two. There is a gap to be crossed but also, in Bultmann's mind, there is a means to cross the gap. The existential interpretation is this means. The process of demythologization which uses it, though difficult to understand in many ways, seems to be intended as a fairly simple and unitary process which will translate between the two cultures and make communication possible. In the more radical position here described, there is apparently no means of crossing it, or at least no unitary, definable and perpetually available means. As we have seen, in Bultmann's thinking the New Testament is still, so long as it is rightly interpreted, the locus through which revelation is mediated; in the newer movement of thought, which I describe, this is no longer so. Finally, seen from the angle of the history of the ideas involved, Bultmann's thought depends not only on existentialism but also on Lutheran theology and on the distinction between the natural sciences with their objectivity and the human sciences with their existential character; cultural relativism as I have described it seems more related to modern social sciences such as sociology and anthropology and the contemporary discussion of their methods.

(iv) Lastly, the kind of radical questioning of the Bible which I have described seems to be naturally accompanied by a high degree of confidence in the church, as the body which provides a continuum for the life of theology and which will be able to make its theological decisions as and when they are needed. The church does not work by any external norm; 'Christianity is a continuing faith which embodies itself',[14] and it will continue to embody itself in the necessary forms to meet future contingencies. It does not require a preordained and ordered programme, with a prescribed 'authority' to which it has to look in moments of uncertainty. This opposition to any systematized and pre-defined prior 'authority' is one of the most striking aspects of this radicalism.

It is too early for us to deliver our own judgment on the validity of this sort of radical opinion of the status of the Bible. But some sort of preliminary reaction of my own may be briefly offered.

(*a*) The strongest side of this radical opinion seems to me to be its protest against the irrationality of ideas of 'biblical authority',

---

[14] The phrase comes from C. F. Evans, *Is 'Holy Scripture' Christian?*, p. 16, but I apply it in a sense which goes beyond his application of it there.

its calling of attention to the accidental and often contradictory character of the process by which the idea of a 'holy scripture' was evolved, its highlighting of the way in which interpreters are forced into artificialities by their need to show the Bible to have been 'in the right'. On all this negative side a strong case has been made, and we are indebted for the honest emphasis of these points.

(*b*) The linking of the case with the position of cultural relativism is much less convincing; it probably introduces contradictions in the radical case which are not necessary to it,[15] and forces it into an extremism which is irrational and self-damaging. Even this, however, is an element which has to be faced by any modern discussion of the place of the Bible, and the question of cultural analogies and differences deserves much more study, to which these arguments have drawn attention.

(*c*) I do not find the arguments advanced by those of this opinion to be very convincing; but I am also aware that it is not easy to find arguments which can refute their opinion in a satisfactory way. This, however, in itself is a sign of the newer position we seem to be reaching: difference over this sort of question within the church seems entirely tolerable. Unlike the men of an earlier age, one does not feel a pressure to confute, one does not feel that at all costs this error must be exposed and silenced. We no longer feel that, in the midst of all sorts of differences within Christianity, at least the nature or source of ultimate authority must be agreed and held in common; we are content to co-exist without this.

(*d*) It remains, however, quite uncertain to what kind of constructive theological position the views which I have been outlining can lead. Their own refusal to offer any structure of priorities or authorities, or any programme for procedure, is indeed bound to leave the future constructive possibilities very vague. With this I am personally not unhappy, for it seems to me that in the future we shall judge theologies not by their antecedent criterion but by their output, their results. Where the authority of the Bible is so completely relativized, we have the right to ask what the positive affirmations of such a theology will be. Will it be a theology of complete relativization? Or will it, in relativizing the Bible, find firm ground by taking some other element and making it absolute – some such other element as the church of today, or the cultural situation of

[15] Cf. further below, pp. 72f.

today, or the natural theology possible for today?[16] But if this is so, then will not these firm elements – the modern church, modern culture, or a modern natural theology – be found on a rigorous analysis to be subject to the same relativity, contingency and irrationality or even absurdity which has been found to attach to the traditional role of the Bible?

Meanwhile, then, we have to wait and see what the positive theological outcome of present radicalism towards the Bible will be; but my feeling is that, when the result is finally there to be observed and assessed, it will be seen to have contradicted some of the preliminary positions now being put forward.

[16] Cf. the interest in natural theology shown by C. F. Evans in his *Is 'Holy Scripture' Christian?*, e.g. pp. 47ff., 98–105.

IV

THE BIBLE AS LITERATURE

It will be convenient to introduce at this point our discussion of the Bible as a work of literature. This is so for two reasons. First of all, while all would doubtless agree that the Bible is in some sense an impressive work of literature, many would think that its status as literature is the lowest level of its functioning, and that the real problems of the Bible as a basic document of Christianity begin only after we leave its character as literature and go on to other levels of the subject. Secondly, there is a connection between the view of the Bible as a literary work and the arguments of the radical questioners, which have been set out in part in the previous chapter.

Various religions, various forms of human society and various types of collective consciousness can be said to refer themselves to some basic story or body of literature which is their foundation myth. In Christianity, as also in Judaism, this foundation myth is constituted by the Bible, which in this sense is somewhat comparable with the place taken by Homer among the Greeks. The Bible is the basic story or document which is read or recited or referred to at almost all meetings of the community and which deeply informs the minds of its members, providing them with pictures, types and categories through which they organize their experience. Sir Walter Scott in his novels, to name but one example, showed how profoundly the mind of the Scottish people had come to be moulded by the phrases and imageries of scripture, which constituted for them the basic intellectual map, to which reference could be had for the placing, identifying or describing of almost any kind of situation or experience. In Scott's work, indeed, this is most obvious in his characterizing of simple Bible-quoting Presbyterian zealots; but something of the same thing, the use of the

Bible as a recognized literary centre round which all sorts of experience could be organized, can be seen in a great deal of English literature (and, doubtless, equally in other Western literature). Thus we may cite Hardy's

> The sadness of Fanny Robin's fate did not make Bathsheba's glorious, although she was the Esther to this poor Vashti . . .

Or in Kipling:

> There be triple ways to take, of the eagle or the snake,
>   Or the way of a man with a maid;
> But the sweetest way to me is a ship's upon the sea
>   In the heel of the North-East Trade.

(Cf. Prov. 30, 18f. [AV]:

> There be three things which are too wonderful for me, yea, four which I know not: The way of an eagle in the air; the way of a serpent upon a rock; the way of a ship in the midst of the sea; and the way of a man with a maid.)

In a writer of deep religious insight like T. S. Eliot the biblical imagery is ubiquitous; sometimes it is explicitly declared as such and explained, sometimes it is more subliminal:

> Lady, three white leopards sat under a juniper-tree
> In the cool of the day . . .

(Cf. I Kings 19.4 [AV]:

> But he himself [Elijah] went a day's journey into the wilderness, and came and sat down under a juniper tree; and he requested for himself that he might die; and said, It is enough; now, O Lord, take away my life, for I am not better than my fathers.)

or again:

>   And the bones sang chirping
> With the burden of the grasshopper, saying . . .

(Cf. Eccles. 12.5 [AV]:

> And the grasshopper shall be a burden, and desire shall fail; because man goeth to his long home, and the mourners go about the streets.)

The point, in fact, need not be laboured. As a literary work, the Bible has been a supreme source of inspiration and imagery; it has been one of the basic underlying 'myths' of our literature, perhaps indeed the most important such myth.[1]

Now it should not be necessary to explain here that I am not using *myth* as a derogatory term meaning 'untrue story' or 'fabrication'; I use it as a literary category. We can perhaps distinguish between two sorts of writing. The first is intended as informational; its value can be assessed from the accuracy of its reports about entities ('referents', things referred to) in the outside world. The second has a different kind of meaning and value. Its meaning lies rather in the structure and shape of the story, and in the images used within it. It is valued as literature, aesthetically, rather than as information.

The meaning of literary myth does not lie in the real existence, in the outside world, of the persons and incidents of the story, and still less is it dependent on the exact accuracy of the description of them. Much of literature, to put it bluntly, is fiction. The efficacy and profundity of the Homeric epics does not at all depend on the real existence of Zeus or Poseidon, or indeed on that of Achilles or Odysseus, or indeed on the question whether there ever was or was not any Greek expedition to Troy. There are indeed human actualities to which the poems appeal and which they help to illuminate and organize, but these actualities are other than the persons or incidents to which they make overt reference.

Why then should it not be so with the Bible also? Why should we not consider the Bible as a literary work of supreme and classic quality, which influences and patterns our lives through the stories it tells and the images it uses, independently of the question whether things happened in fact as they are related in the Bible, and independently of the question whether the entities mentioned in the Bible have any objective existence? In other words, to put it again in a crude form, what if we were to think of the Bible as a supremely profound work of fiction?

(*a*) There have always been certain portions of the Bible which seem to call for interpretation along these lines. The book of Job,

---

[1] Cf. Northrop Frye, *Anatomy of Criticism* (London: Oxford University Press, 1957), p. 140: 'the Bible, the main source for undisplaced myth in our tradition'. For the sense of *undisplaced*, see Frye's explanations on pp. 139f.

for instance, is one portion in which the truly literary character is most manifest. The effect which it produces, and the profundity of its handling of problems, are in no way dependent on its correctness as reportage of externally existing persons or events. It makes no difference whether there was a Job or an Eliphaz, whether there was or is a Satan; even to ask the question, as if something important depended on it, would be to show one's failure to understand the sort of literature that this is. Job is an outstanding example of a biblical book which has to be evaluated as literature.

But this appreciation does not apply only to Job. In the Gospels parables are common, and a parable, if taken at the level of its direct referential meaning, is a fictional story. There was no Good Samaritan or Prodigal Son, and it makes no difference whether there was or not. The message of the parable is something other than the story which it itself tells.

These stories, of course, commonly have the term *parable* applied to them explicitly in the New Testament, and for this reason their non-informational character has generally been recognized. In modern times, however, people have begun to extend the same sort of understanding to some other biblical stories which do not call themselves parables; thus, for instance, it has become fairly common practice to say that the book of Jonah is in this sense a parable. The whale or fish thus becomes part of the furniture of the story and has no more objective existence than the coin worth thousands of pounds which a man buried in his garden, because he thought that he was supposed to preserve it and not to invest it at interest.

The book of Jonah is, no doubt, a marginal case, to which few attach central importance, and the same might be true of Job. But the principle can be extended to more important materials. Take the structure of the creation story in Genesis, with the sequence of stages over six or seven days. Our forefathers took this to refer to a sequence which had objective reality in the outside world; the world had in fact originated in such a sequence. Within Christianity this is not now generally believed. We are now told that the story tells us something about God, something about the nature of man, perhaps also indirectly something about the world as it is related to God; but it certainly does not tell us how the world came into existence. The story is thus in fact viewed as a sort of fiction, the purport of which is something quite other than its surface meaning.

But if the creation story can be considered thus, cannot the same be said of the story of Jesus' birth, or the story of his resurrection, or that of the exodus of the Israelites from Egypt? Do not all of these stories work upon us in the same way as general literature does? And do they not exercise their power upon us quite apart from the question whether things happened as they are narrated in the external world? Is not their effect upon us essentially the same as that exercised by the myths, the patterns, the imagery and the symbols of all great literature?

With this we have plainly come to the point of some major problems in the functioning of the Bible within Christian faith.

(*b*) If biblical stories and poems work upon people in the same way as the myths and imagery of general literature, and not through their referential informational function in telling about events and entities in the outside world, this should not be put down to scepticism or unbelief. I am not saying that people refuse to believe the biblical stories as they stand and therefore, rather than regard them as mere lies or follies, are forced to interpret them parabolically. This is at most a small part of the process which has occurred. If the creation story of Genesis is increasingly regarded as somewhat parabolic, while its surface credibility has decreased, it would be crude to suppose that the simple incredulity came first and was then followed by an adoption of the parabolic understanding. The latter is felt by people to be an enrichment of faith rather than a consequence of scepticism; it seems to them to direct faith more truly towards its real object, namely the understanding of God and man, and helpfully dissociates it from past false entanglements with an ancient cosmogony. It can thus happen, not only in Genesis but in the Bible as a whole, that the parabolic, mythical or literary mode of impact is experienced as the primary one, and this mode of impact becomes antecedent to the question of what actually happened or what external realities are referred to. Not only is it antecedent to these questions, but the effect seems to be similar however they are answered. Thus, if people say that the story of Jesus' birth is a kind of myth, this should not be ascribed to simple refusal to believe in the possibility of a virgin birth. The sense is rather that the story has its main effect anyway before the question of historical events or external realities is answered; and that, even when this latter question has been answered, it has not added to the effectiveness of the story.

Thus, in general, if we talk about the Bible as a kind of literary myth of Christianity, we are not by any means describing some sort of scepticism or unbelief; we are talking about the situation in which many believing Christians are, and which has been brought upon them through the tradition of biblical interpretation and of theology.

(*c*) One factor in this is that Christian faith today shows very substantial latitude and variation in what is believed about matters like the creation of the world, the birth of Jesus and his resurrection. In what sense do we say that the world was created by God, or that God raised Jesus from the dead? Apart from particular segments of Christianity like fundamentalism, answers to such questions are either vague or various. The effect of the biblical passage on the average church-goer is more that of the literary myth and less that of a deliberate doctrine about the things to be believed. But though a majority of serious Christians can have only vague beliefs about such matters, it is noticeable that many of them become quite seriously disturbed by real scepticism when they hear it expressed. This suggests perhaps that the positive effect of the passages is that of the literary myth, while the effect of scepticism is to damage the attractiveness of the myth and at the same time to drag people suddenly back to a doctrinal and referential understanding of the passages, which they then feel they have either to defend or to abandon.

(*d*) Another factor which works in the same direction is the liturgical or devotional mode in which the Bible is so largely used in the life of the churches. Much reading of the Bible takes place in a liturgical context, and liturgy contains an immense amount of biblical phraseology. The interrelation between Bible and liturgy varies from one tradition to another: in Anglicanism, for instance, there is a great deal of Bible reading in the service, along with much liturgical use very close to the Bible, while the amount of explicit exposition by preaching is often quite small; in some other traditions one finds much scriptural exposition in a sermon but much less in liturgy, but as complement to this a tradition of personal devotional reading which comes close to the liturgical in its myth-related character. The liturgical or devotional use of the Bible appears to accentuate the idea of its reapplicability to new situations, the notion of it as a treasury of imagery usable again and again, a sort of divinely-given poetry in which the church of all ages can express itself and understand itself. But this kind of usage can leave it unclear just how far the biblical stories depend for their value on referential content, on objective external facts to which they refer. The more one hears of the exodus of Israel from Egypt as part of the liturgy for the baptism of infants in water, the less one is concerned to ask whether any Israelites ever came out of Egypt and, if they did, how they got out.

(*e*) The liturgical-devotional use of the Bible seems thus to fit in with the idea that it works as a central literary myth. In more traditional theological terms, this use appears to involve a great deal of typology and allegorization.[2] The Bible provides a series of types or categories of powerful literary character, and these characterize the Christian experience and mark out its distinctive features. Scholars have indeed often had doubts about the typological use of the Bible, and they have opposed the allegorical use of it even more strongly, but these strictures have often exempted the liturgical and devotional use of the Bible, and even the homiletical use of it.[3] We shall not pursue this further, but note only that the liturgical and devotional use of the Bible, implying the applicability of its language to all sorts and conditions of men at all times, points in favour of its function as a store of myth and imagery for Christianity.

(*f*) A purely literary reading of the Bible is something that the church can hope to share with society as a whole. In so far as the Bible is read at all by persons who are not of religious faith, it is likely to be read purely as a literary work, just as they might read Homer. They may well read it without feeling any necessity to go on and ask the more specifically theological questions about the events related or the entities referred to. Such literary appreciation

[2] These are sometimes distinguished, on the ground that *typology* is an analogy between historical persons or situations, while *allegory* moves away from historical relations into relations entirely unhistorical and metaphysical. The distinction is not important for my argument, since I consider the two to be rather interwoven; see my *Old and New in Interpretation*, esp. pp. 103–48.

[3] E.g. G. W. H. Lampe in *Essays on Typology* (London: SCM Press, 1957), p. 35, rejects the 'kind of typology which rests upon artificial and unhistorical correspondences' and holds that it cannot provide genuine exegesis or proof of doctrine; it may however 'find a place in sermon illustrations'.

of the Bible in our culture should be looked on positively by the church and highly valued by it.

In the past there has been some tendency to suppose that the theological use of the Bible must be something quite different from its literary appreciation, or that the latter stood on a much lower level than the former.[4] This, however, we have just seen to be unlikely; within Christian faith itself the functioning of the Bible in certain respects has close affinities to the literary appreciation of it.[5] The past position of the Bible in our culture is one of the ways in which Jewish-Christian faith has affected our world, and the study of the Bible as literature is a proper recognition of this fact. Conversely, such study of the Bible is an important potential point of contact for the future relations of religion and culture. It is sometimes said that the Bible is supposed to be studied and interpreted 'within the church' (whatever that may mean), but this seems to be a wrong emphasis: the Bible is study material for the world as a whole and not for the church only; it is work for schools, education colleges and universities, for historians and literary scholars, as well as for clergymen and theologians. It is to the interest of Christian faith that knowledge and appreciation of the Bible in our culture should be at a high level, even if its nature is entirely non-theological or even sceptical, just as it is to the interest of the church that the atheism and agnosticism in the community should also be of the highest intellectual standard.

We should recognize however that there is in the culture, and not only in the church, a certain reluctance to see the Bible as a work of literature. If the Bible is not read, this is paradoxically because it is supposed to be 'true', i.e. to be true in the referential sense in which Homer or *Hamlet* is not true. The older Christian tradition, especially in its controversial statements (which may well differ, as has been implied above, from the actual function of the Bible in worship), has valued the Bible not as literature but predominantly as true information. This being so, and this insistence having made deep marks within the culture, those who no longer

[4] Some persons of literary renown have themselves expressed doubt about the value or extent of a literary, as distinct from a theological, reading of the Bible; but we can respect this opinion without necessarily sharing it. See T. R. Henn, 'The Bible as Literature', in *Peake's Commentary on the Bible* (2nd edition, Edinburgh: Nelson, 1962), pp. 8–23.

[5] Conversely, we should consider the possibility that great literature possesses a kind of theological dimension of its own.

accept the Bible as true information react by not reading it at all. Thus, in spite of the literary merits of the Bible and its important cultural heritage, we find students studying (say) English literature who are quite ignorant about the Bible, who may have no idea who Job, or Lot, or Nicodemus were, and who consider the Bible to lie beyond the horizon of their work in a way they would not treat any other comparable body of material.

We may perhaps hope, however, that this situation will improve and that more people will come to experience the Bible as literature, partly because the pressure for a 'theological' reading of the Bible will begin to fade as memories of the older cultural state die away.

(*g*) In any case, as we have seen, it is not possible to make an absolute distinction between a theological use of the Bible and a literary appreciation of it. Certain of the characteristics of the Bible, when read simply as literature, are in fact reproduced in certain types of Christian use of the Bible. The issues in this will be clarified if we consider the various processes of study which are involved.

Three possible processes of study of the Bible

Study of entities referred to
Referential

A

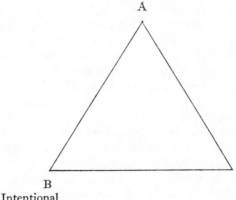

B
Intentional

Study of mind of
the writers

C
Poetic or
aesthetic

Study of myths
and images of
the text as it is

It might be possible to set some approaches to the Bible in the figure of a triangle. At one corner (A) we would set the quest for the entities referred to. Of these entities, the referents of the biblical text, some could be called theological entities: God, heaven, and so on (whether these are real entities or not does not concern us at this point). Others would rather be historical entities: the wars of such and such a king, the details of the Roman government in Palestine. These latter entities are often historical events with a theological value; we do not divide entities into two classes, either theological or historical; but historical entities will be material for the historian, though they may also be material for the theologian. In any case all study in this corner of the triangle is study in the entities to which the Bible refers, the persons or events of which it speaks. At a second corner (B) we have a study of the persons who wrote the books, and the quest for what was in their minds. What did they *intend* when they wrote this or that? What were their personal circumstances, what were the motives and interests which impelled them? When did they live? Were they really the persons who are traditionally supposed to have written the books? All study in this corner is study in the persons from whom the Bible emanated, their purposes and their mentality or their theology. At the third corner (C) we have the forms and patterns of the biblical text as it is. Study in this corner is directed towards these patterns – their effect as imagery, their relations to the overall shape of the Bible. Such study is interested in the poetic, aesthetic or mythopoeic quality of the Bible, as a literary work, just as it is.

This triangular distinction between different modes of study of the Bible is, however, comparatively new. In the older Christendom the three were all rolled up in one. The Bible offered a unity of myth and aesthetic pattern, extended throughout the Bible and the world by the typological and allegorical style of interpretation; but it was not supposed that anyone would savour this myth and pattern as a purely aesthetic experience, for any reader of the Bible was expected also to accept it as an account of actual entities and events – entities like God, events like the exodus of Israel from Egypt, the crossing of the Red Sea, the rising of Jesus from the dead. And as for the motivation and the ideas or intellectual ancestry of the writers, this was a minor matter, since in essence the Bible came from God. It was indeed a product of human agency; but one would not explain it as a result of human ideas and human motivations, since the human agents had in essence got their material from God. It is only in the modern world that the three modes of study have broken apart.

The modern scholarly expositor of the Bible works primarily, it would seem, in the second mode; he concerns himself not with the flat literary relations on the surface of the biblical text as it is, but with the intentions of the writer in his historical setting. It is within this process of study that historical criticism has come into being, and one of its implications has been the breakdown of the old typological and allegorical interpretations, and therefore the breakdown of the unity of the Bible as it was once conceived, the unity of a seamless robe, a network of interrelated images. Thus biblical scholarship has tended to draw apart not only from the old traditional Christian understanding of scripture but also from the general aesthetic appreciation of literature as we would apply it, let us say, to Homer or to Shakespeare. The separation can be illustrated by the different usages of the term *literary criticism*, which in general literary study is a study of the structures and imagery of works, their modes, symbols and myths, while in biblical scholarship it is used for source analysis, the separating out of the historically different layers in composite works.

But if historical scholarship has split apart the older unity of the Bible, can such a unity be found again in a new basis? In fact the revival of the idea of biblical authority in this century carried with it an emphasis on the unity of the Bible; it was indeed, some suggested, the Bible as a whole that had authority, not particular parts of it. Moreover, the same period saw a certain attempt to revive typological methods of interpretation which, as we have seen, are a mode of understanding the Bible as a unity and indeed the whole of life as a unity with the biblical patterns at its centre. Yet it must be added that both these movements in their twentieth-century form, both the interest in the unity of the Bible and the interest in typology, carefully avoided negating the historical method of study; rather, they represented an attempt at synthesis over and above that historical method.[6] They cannot therefore be regarded as full realizations of an approach to the Bible as literature or as myth. Moreover we have seen that the popularity of this emphasis on the unity of the Bible has seriously waned.

It may well be asked, however, whether the time is now coming

[6] Cf. for instance C. F. Evans, op. cit., pp. 32f. etc.

when a more fully literary study of the Bible will begin to assert itself, a study which will really concern itself with the imagery and structure of the text as it stands, probably ruling out as irrelevant for this purpose the historical and intentional concerns which have dominated technical biblical scholarship.[7] In fact considerable work is now being carried out which strives to bring biblical study closer to the methods of the general appreciation of literature.[8] It is not yet clear however what the implications of these new lines of study will be for the status of the Bible as a holy book.

Positively, such studies will be likely to elucidate, in a way which present-day professional biblical scholarship does not, the way in which the myths and images of the Bible act upon the general

[7] Since readers may ask themselves the question, I would say that procedures like form criticism and redaction criticism, in spite of some differences from documentary source criticism, belong for the most part together with it as historical in interest. They are pursued very largely with the purpose of getting at the movement of the tradition in the time before the present form of the text was reached, or of getting at the processes by which it was reached. In this respect they are historical and intentional; they ask what was the mental process which produced this text. What I call a fully literary approach would ask rather what is the meaning of this text as it is. On this cf. a work, the effect of which on biblical study has hardly yet begun, W. K. Wimsatt's 'The Intentional Fallacy', in his *The Verbal Icon* (paperback, New York: Noonday Press, 1962), pp. 2–18.

[8] The literature is expanding rapidly. See M. Weiss, *The Bible and Modern Literary Theory* (in Hebrew; Jerusalem, 2nd edn., 1967), and his contribution at the Uppsala Old Testament Congress, *Vetus Testamentum Supplements* xxii (1972); also considerable literary analysis of the Bible by Israeli scholars in periodicals like *Ha-Sifrut*. French structuralism is certain to make a large contribution, and see P. Beauchamp, *Création et séparation* (Paris, 1969), and his contribution at Uppsala, *Vetus Testamentum Supplements* xxii (1972); also M. Lane, *Structuralism: a Reader* (London: Cape, 1970), including E. Leach's article 'The Legitimacy of Solomon', pp. 248–92; and cf. J. Rogerson, 'Structural Anthropology and the Old Testament', *BSOAS* xxxiii (1970), pp. 490–500; in Germany, cf. W. Richter, *Exegese als Literaturwissenschaft* (Göttingen, 1971), and the review by H. Barth and O. H. Steck, *Exegese des Alten Testaments: Leitfaden der Methodik* (2nd edn., 1971), pp. 104–8; F. Alonso-Schökel, *Estudios de poética hebrea* (Barcelona, 1963), and his *The Inspired Word* (London: Burns and Oates, 1967), with my review in *Religious Studies* v (1970). For a rather crushing judgment by a literary critic on the literary ability of biblical scholars see R. M. Frye's paper on 'A Literary Perspective for the Criticism of the Gospels' in *Jesus and Man's Hope* (Pittsburgh Festival on the Gospels: Pittsburgh, 1971), ii, pp. 193–221.

reader. They are likely also to be of help in the restoration of the Bible as a basic literary monument of interest to those who are without any religious interest. On the other side, these studies may turn out to be theologically neutral, and this indeed is one reason why they are likely to be helpful to those who read without themselves having a religious interest.

Negatively, these studies may have a reactionary effect towards the whole structure of historical biblical criticism; they may treat it at best as irrelevant, and they may find a welcome in the minds of those who are strange or hostile towards its methods and results. The study of the Bible as literature might then result in a kind of unholy alliance between a quite secular and non-theological study on the one hand, and on the other hand the prejudices of all those who out of religious motives are hostile to historical criticism.

Before going further, we should not fail to note that there is a difference between the appreciation of the Bible as literature and its use in liturgy and devotional reading. In this chapter the two have been rather taken together, because certain common mental attitudes seem to be discernible: in particular, the idea of a *myth* underlying a literature, and the liturgical celebration of a foundation myth in a religion, seem to be comparable. In both cases, we may remark, there is a certain continuity between such modern use of the Bible and the mode within which it originated. At least some parts of the Bible may reasonably be thought to have grown up in the first place as folk literature or court literature: such, let us suppose, would be the J and E stories of the Pentateuch, the Succession Story of David, the Song of Songs, the older Wisdom collections of Proverbs – which include, we may note, some of the finest literary material of the Bible. But many other parts owed their very origin and primeval function to liturgical contexts: the Psalms themselves are the most obvious example. And it was the liturgical context into which the books as a whole were eventually integrated: they became texts for regular reading in the setting of worship, in synagogue or church. To say that they are 'holy scripture' is in effect to recognize them as official texts for this purpose. The literary and the liturgical character of the Bible thus have much in common, both in the origin of the Bible and in the mode of its operation.

Nevertheless it would be wrong to ignore important differences between literary and liturgical uses of the Bible. Literary appreciation may be occasional; use in worship is regular and recurrent. Literary reading will normally imply the starting at the beginning of a book, which is the normal literary unit, and reading on to the end of it; but liturgy, while reading certain passages (usually something from ten verses to a chapter in length), also uses an intricate web of allusions from all over the Bible, tying together passages from all sorts of sources and thus using a kind of harmonizing procedure. Though certain aspects of liturgical use of scripture fit in well with a literary, aesthetic appreciation of imagery, this is not – at least on most views of liturgy – its sole or its main function: the Bible is used in worship also referentially, to call attention to a divine reality which is believed to have real existence. And, correspondingly, the reading of scripture in worship (or in private devotional reading) has a strong *moral* aspect: it is edifying, it is religiously improving, it brings before us that which is right, it leads us into communion with God, into the sharing of his mind towards us.

In other words, if I have introduced liturgy and devotional reading here, in connection with the use of the Bible as literature, we have to go on to see it also as part of the use of the Bible as information and as theology, which will be dealt with in following chapters. If one can distinguish between different intellectual processes in which the Bible is used and comprehended, its liturgical and devotional use would seem to comprehend and touch upon all of these processes. It is for this reason that no separate chapter has been devoted to the place of the Bible in liturgy and devotion.

In any case, my knowledge of liturgical matters is scanty, and I know nothing about the current discussions of possible liturgical reform. In that sense I have rather taken the liturgical situation as it is and accepted it as such. Whether, for instance, in view of present discussions, or in view even of the arguments of this book, the place of the Bible in the worship of the churches ought to be rethought; whether it might be somewhat withdrawn from liturgical use and used in a different type of context and study – such questions have not emerged in the studies in which I have taken part and I shall not attempt to handle them here. Certain points in the argument that follows, however, will have reference back to the setting of the Bible in worship and liturgy.[9]

[9] See below, pp. 136, 138.

In sum, then, I do not wish to make any premature or excessive identification between the literary appreciation of the Bible and the liturgical use of it. All I suggest at this point is that there are certain common aspects between these two, and that these common aspects form an important link between the literary understanding, which might otherwise be an entirely secular approach, and a traditional Christian mode of use of the Bible.

There remain two other aspects in which literary appreciation has been particularly connected with the modern discussion of the status of the Bible, and to these we shall now turn. In both cases there has been some discussion between the views of theologians and those of prominent literary scholars, and we can expect this exchange to be fruitful.

The first approach to the Bible among these two is one which well illustrates the linkage between literary and liturgical sense discussed above. I refer to the approach best known from the work of Austin Farrer and Lionel Thornton, the approach which Alan Richardson justly entitles 'the theology of images'.[10] If I understand it rightly, this way of thinking views the Bible as essentially poetic and symbolic in nature. Scripture does not proceed by systematic argument nor by the giving of information about historical facts. Typological or allegorical methods are taken to underlie the work of the biblical writers, and this provides the key to detailed exegesis: it can uncover the symbolism in all sorts of details, such as the number of loaves or fishes, or the significance of a piece of clothing in the Gospels. Thus Mark's 'whole Gospel is a great and complex symbol of the Resurrection'.[11]

This poetic and symbolic approach is not only the key to the sense of the biblical books but also the way in which they can be regarded as revelatory. There is here revealed truth 'not as a matter of intellectual propositions but as reality apprehended by the imagination'.[12] According to this approach, Hodgson writes, 'it is the presentation in images that makes the Bible revelatory and . . . if we would receive God's revelation we must think in images too.'[13]

[10] A. Richardson, *The Bible in the Age of Science*, title of ch. 7; see especially pp. 158–63.

[11] Gardner, *The Business of Criticism*, p. 113.

[12] Richardson, op. cit., p. 162.

[13] In Hodgson, *Authority*, p. 95 (from citation by Nineham).

Can such a view of the status of the Bible, based on its character as imagery and symbol, be accepted?

(*a*) As exegesis the work of Dr Farrer and others like him has not proved itself; to biblical scholars generally it appears fanciful, extreme and at times idiosyncratic to a point approaching fantasy. It would be most unwise for the church to accept as fundamental any view of the status of the Bible which rested on so thin and so controverted a line of exegetical procedure.

(*b*) From at least some literary critics also this approach has undergone severe criticism, and I have in mind, of course, the studies of Helen Gardner in particular – whose objections are all the stronger in that they are fundamentally in agreement with the objections voiced by the professional biblical scholar. To sum up with one of her own sentences, 'As literary criticism I cannot regard the new symbolical or typological approach to the Gospels as satisfactory.'[14]

(*c*) It could be replied, however, that these are criticisms not against the *principle*, but against a particular *embodiment*, of a poetic and symbolic approach to the Bible. If the work had been better done, and done in a way more in accord with the thinking of professional biblical scholars, might it not have proved itself? No one doubts, after all, that typology is a real element within the Bible; and, even if there is not as much of it as was imagined by Dr Farrer, does it not have to be appreciated as such and be accorded due weight in the argument for a poetic and symbolic account of the Bible?

Against this one might reply: (i) the extent of typology in the Bible is considerable, but is still (as seen under the control of responsible biblical scholarship) distinctly limited; it is therefore not so completely dominating that it can in itself justify the principle of a poetic and symbolic approach as *the* universal and overarching expression of the status of the Bible; (ii) biblical typology itself can hardly be adequately expressed as a cultivation of images and symbols; it is very commonly rather a recourse to something valued as historical, as legally binding, as 'revealed truth';[15] thus the fact of biblical typology can be evaluated histori-

[14] Gardner, op. cit., p. 126.
[15] The whole 'theology of images' can be seen as one particular position taken in that stage of theological discussion in which great importance was attached to the question of revelation, and in which therefore the question

cally by us, as a part of the mental make-up of the men of the Bible (or some of them),[16] but it is not sufficient to validate *for us* an approach through images and symbols as *the* essential mode of appreciation of the Bible.

(*d*) From another theological point of view, the approach under discussion can be criticized for trying to pick out and absolutize the poetic and symbolic character of the Bible as *the* element which is the bearer of revelation. In spite of the labyrinthine complexity of the imagery itself as expounded by scholars like Farrer, this can lead in the end to a simplistic account of the theological status of the Bible. This criticism has already been voiced by Nineham.[17] To localize the authority of the Bible uniquely in the imagery might be as deleterious as to localize it uniquely in the theological propositions or in the historical events reported.

This then is one of the recent discussions which have involved relations between literary appreciation and theological evaluation of the Bible. We now pass however to another, which has some points of contact with that just mentioned, and which is also related to the matter of cultural relativism, discussed earlier.[18] Dr Nineham is one of those who have laid particular emphasis on the lessons to be learned by theologians and biblical scholars from the general appreciation of literature, and I quote *in extenso* a recent passage on the subject:[19]

> Modern literary critics are agreed about the impropriety of trying to isolate and state '*the* meaning' of the type of writing they study. Thus Professor Helen Gardner, for example, praises Miss Mary Lascelles's book on *Measure for Measure* precisely on the ground that she makes no attempt in it to 'arrive finally at "*the* meaning of *Measure for Measure*". She has been content to leave the play more meaningful than it was before we read her study.' Those words are a quotation and they refer, be it noted, to a single dramatic work by a single author. The Bible too

---

of 'revealed truths' or 'revelation of propositions' was much discussed; see again below, pp. 123–6.

[16] On this in general see my *Old and New in Interpretation*, ch. 4, 'Typology and Allegory', where I have presented my views on this matter at greater length.

[17] In Hodgson, *Authority*, p. 95.

[18] See above, pp. 38–52.

[19] Nineham, *BJRL* lii (1969), p. 184.

contains dramatic work and it contains much poetry, parable and what I may call symbolic writing of many other kinds; it was composed over a period of a millennium or more by many writers of very different characters, beliefs and cultural backgrounds. If nevertheless we are to maintain that there is something which can be called '*the* meaning' of the Bible that will surely be an act of faith; the existence in the Bible of such a coherent meaning will be due to the providential activity of God, and the guidance of the Holy Spirit will be necessary in order to discover what it is.

This argument, though I have cited it in full, does not display the full ramifications of Dr Nineham's analogy from literary appreciation, nor are the consequences for the idea of authority fully spelled out. The following points can be made in comment on the passage cited:

(*a*) There is an important point which bears on the importance of all comment on literary works. In so far as a work is really literary and not merely informational in its scope and character, it can perhaps be said *to be its own meaning*,[20] or to set forth its own meaning. For a work to be literary in character means that it does not have a detachable meaning which might have been stated in some other way; the way in which it was stated in the work is in fact the 'message' or the 'meaning' of this work. Any comment on such works can therefore aim only at elucidating the work and sending the reader back to the work itself; it cannot hope to encapsulate the meaning in another set of words. The result of all the accumulated scholarship expended on St Mark will then be that the reader, his mind illuminated by all this, will seek the end-product, the meaning of the gospel, by reading: St Mark. This opinion seems to me in itself entirely correct. The question which arises from it for the use of the Bible in the church is only this: which books or sections of the Bible count as 'literary' material in this regard, and which count as informational.[21]

[20] Cf. R. M. Frye, *Perspective on Man: Literature and the Christian Tradition* (Philadelphia: Westminster Press, 1961), p. 43: 'A literary work *is* its own meaning, and its meaning cannot be univocally abstracted from it. This is the one literary principle upon which all competent literary critics now agree.'

[21] One might thus think of (let us say) the letters of St Paul as 'occasional' rather than 'literary' works in this sense; the test being that one could have gone to him and asked him to restate his meaning in other

(*b*) It is not so clear, however, against what Dr Nineham is directing his strictures on any idea of '*the* meaning'. The phrase '*the* meaning' (with stress on the definite article) is not much found in the writings of biblical scholars or theologians. The more obvious exegesis of Nineham's paragraph is this: one cannot state *the* meaning of a play by a unitary and known author; *a fortiori*, one cannot state *the* meaning of a composite and disparate collection like the Bible; if it can be done at all, it can be done only by an act of faith (it is not clear to me whether Dr Nineham considers this to be a good thing or not); being done by an act of faith, it cannot rest upon exact exegetical scholarship. But, beyond this, Dr Nineham's argument seems to confuse several different things:

(i) His first point refers to the undesirability of stating 'the' meaning of any literary work; this we have discussed above.

(ii) His second point is, it seems, a passing over into another genus, for he is now treating of the *composite* character of the Bible, the problem of its coherence, and the question whether it has tried to 'communicate the whole tradition of doctrine necessary to salvation'.[22] This seems to me to be not a natural advance from the previous point established, but a switch to a quite other set of questions.

(iii) Thirdly, Dr Nineham, within the total context of his article, gives the impression that any idea of '*the* authority' of '*the* Bible' depends logically on the idea that '*the* meaning' of this Bible can be stated; but it is not clear where the argument goes from here. Does it mean that the statement of '*the* meaning' cannot be done on an exegetical basis at all, but will require an appeal to the crassly supernatural? Or does it mean that a 'coherent meaning' of the Bible cannot be expressed in human terms, though 'the guidance of the Holy Spirit' will enable us to discern it. I confess myself somewhat at a loss in seeking to follow this part of the argument.

(*c*) It is probable that the argument also leads in another direction. There are, it suggests, all sorts of meanings but no one mean-

---

words, and that he could have done this (indeed, may very probably have done so); it is not so clear that one could have done this with the Gospel writers, who might have had to take the viewpoint of 'what I have written, I have written'.

[22] Nineham, ibid., p. 185; see the entire paragraph which follows the one quoted by me. Here Dr Nineham seems (mistakenly in my opinion) to suppose that statements about 'the' meaning imply that the Bible was carefully planned to include a summary of all necessary doctrine.

ing which is *the* meaning. You can discern this kind of meaning and you can discern that kind of meaning, but you have no right ever to say that any of this wide range of possibilities is *the* meaning. Some poets, according to Dame Helen Gardner, 'when asked what their poems mean, reply that they mean what anyone can make of them'.[23] If I read Dr Nineham's mind aright, then, his argument is for multiplicity of meaning and against the attempt to *determine* meaning. It must be doubted, however, whether literary critics in fact assume so easy-going and tolerant a view of all the 'meanings' which have been found in literary works by other literary critics. F. R. Leavis, for instance, does not give us the impression of a discipline in which all sorts of meanings can be 'found', all of which have then to be tolerantly received as part of a variegated picture, on the ground that meanings cannot be defined and multiplicity of meanings is the normal thing. Helen Gardner, as we have seen, in the same work in which she praises Miss Lascelles so highly, is herself engaged in an attempt to dissuade readers from acceptance of the symbolic and typological approach advocated by Farrer.

(*d*) Perhaps however an intermediate position can be stated. The literary critic, shall we say, finds it possible to make certain negative discriminations, to say that, whatever the meaning is, it is not what is supposed in such and such a suggestion. By ruling out certain possibilities a fence of possible positive meaning is drawn around the text. But within this area there is still a high degree of indeterminacy; having excluded certain 'wrong' suggestions, one does not go on to seek a definition of the one 'right' meaning. Something very similar to this, one may suppose, is done in biblical exegesis: linguistic or historical evidence rules out such and such an interpretation, but a number of possible constructions remain to be considered within the area remaining. Such a position would permit a wide range of possible meanings while still retaining the power to deny particular alleged interpretations.

(*e*) In another part of the same lecture Dr Nineham limits in another way the possibility of defining meaning. Here he seems to maintain that, even if we know what the Bible *meant* (in the past, in its own setting), this does not tell us what it means now: indeed, it may have to be admitted that it does not have any meaning at all today. 'Many statements in ancient texts have *no* meaning today in any normal sense of the word "meaning".'[24] This brings us back

[23] Gardner, ibid., p. 113.   [24] Nineham, *BJRL*, ibid., p. 181.

to a kind of cultural relativism: a work composed in an ancient culture has its meaning in that culture, and in our culture may have a different meaning, or indeed no meaning at all.[25]

We have already discussed some of the aspects of this view, and here I would only add one observation: this view, if correct, appears to run entirely counter to the principle, which Dr Nineham himself supports, of following the analogy of literary appreciation. In literary study the appreciation of works written in the past and in different cultures is a normal daily affair; and there is no reason to suppose that modern works, originating in our own time and culture, are more obvious in their meaning, more transparent or in any other way more meaningful. The reverse is commonly true. At the beginning of this chapter we considered the possibility that the Bible should be understood in the same way as Homer is understood, and one would have expected this proposal to be congenial to Dr Nineham; but it does not fit with the argument we are at present considering, since Homer – being a long time ago and in a different culture – would be if anything more remote than the Bible and likely therefore to be even more meaningless. The argument for cultural relativism, in fact, is deeply in contradiction with the appeal to literary appreciation; such support as it gains must come from a quite other direction.

It is now time to attempt a summing-up of what has emerged from this consideration of the reading of the Bible as literature.

(*a*) It would appear that a study of this kind is indeed likely to give access to some important ways in which the Bible has its effect. These range from the liturgical and devotional use of the Bible to its reading by non-religious people. Moreover, one must grant the essential legitimacy of a type of reading which looks at the text as it stands, its structures, its imagery and its myths.

(*b*) A study of this kind might indeed thus provide an understanding of the Bible as a whole, or at least of whole books or groups of books which form a unit (e.g. the Pentateuch, Luke-Acts). Unless safeguards are provided, however, such a study is in some danger of having a reactionary effect and glossing over what has been accomplished by the historical-critical study of the Bible.

(*c*) Such a study, assuming that it was kept free from becoming a screen for purely reactionary objection to historical criticism,

[25] Cf. above, pp. 10, 38–41.

would be at least in part theologically neutral; and this fact would be one of its advantages for certain purposes. On the other hand the church should probably accept that any form of effectiveness of the Bible as a work read, even if it takes place in a complete ignoring of theological questions, is in fact a way in which the biblical message has its effect upon the world.

But the major limitation in processes of reading the Bible straightforwardly as literature is something else: the poor articulateness of theological discussion that could be achieved if this were the only method of approach. Literary comment will, as we have seen, improve our appreciation of the Bible; but in the end it will simply send us back to the Bible, telling us to read it again and enjoy it more. There are, I submit, theological questions which just cannot be answered, cannot even be approached or posed, on this basis. Is there really a God? Did Jesus come from him? Granted that the Resurrection is the central symbol of a Gospel, does it have existence only within the text of the Gospels, as Setebos has existence only within the text of *The Tempest*, or does it also stand for something in the outside world?

In the discussion of such theological questions material from the purely literary study of the Bible can be helpful; but it is doubtful whether such material can be put forward with the kind of articulateness that is suited for theological discussion. Can one hope to gain much within such discussion from an assessment of the general and total aesthetic impact of St Mark, or of Acts, or of Job? The output from such literary study is not meant to be, and is not likely to be, well adapted for discussion of the theological questions. As we saw at the beginning, there are segments within the Bible, like the book of Job, which even the theological reader reads more or less as fiction; but he is able to do this precisely because these books do not form the central structure of his faith; they serve rather to complement and fill out a central structure which comes from elsewhere. This structure appears to be formed on the basis of two things: either special events, like the birth, the death and the resurrection of Jesus, which are taken as seminal; or passages which are unusually doctrinally articulate. It is on the basis of this last matter that the Pauline writings have achieved so high a status in the formulation of the central doctrinal structure of many forms of Christianity.

V

EVENT AND INTERPRETATION –
THE BIBLE AS INFORMATION

In the previous chapter I discussed the Bible as the classic literary expression or archetype of the Christian experience. Seen in this way, the Bible might appear as a great literary work of almost fictional character, a work in which however we would no more expect to find information about the external world than we would do in enjoying the poems of Homer. The patterns and imagery of the literary text would function to provide forms and categories for the Christian consciousness in its understanding of itself and of the world.

Such a view, we have indicated, certainly has some truth in it; but most readers of the Bible will argue that it is at the most only a small part of the truth, and that the Bible functions in other modes which are more important. The mode regarded as most important is that in which the Bible provides information[1] about events. The Bible, it would be argued, is not only a sublime myth, or a fine literary expression of the classic self-understanding of Judaism and Christianity; it should not be placed on the same level as Homer or Shakespeare, and literary modes of appreciation in themselves do not do it justice. The entities and events referred to in the Bible are not mere characters in a story; they are not personalities, incidents or stage furniture having no existence outside

[1] Some writers use the term 'information' in order to suggest purely factual and neutral data, such as dates, measurements and other cold facts, all profounder reaction being excluded. In view of this, I should simply explain that this is not my usage. 'Information' here includes emotional reactions, religious valuations, personal involvement and so on, provided that this is focused upon an external entity, person or event of which the text in question speaks.

the work, more or less fictional, in which they appear. On the contrary, they are – or some of them are – external realities or entities, and it is the Bible which provides the essential information about these entities; indeed, it may be said, in a more extreme form, it provides the only such information. To appreciate the Bible as sublime literature may or may not be justified, but is in itself quite accidental and is in no way essential to faith; what faith depends upon is the reality of certain persons and events reported in scripture. If these reports are sometimes pretty poor stuff as literature, then so much the better, since literary quality is entirely a side-issue. When we say that the Bible is a document of faith we say that its value does not rest in its own literary quality or effect but in its function as a sign which points beyond itself to the external realities on which faith is based. In other words, in the terms of our diagram of p. 61, the basic function of the Bible is referential; its study belongs to point A of our triangle.

Christian faith is not a set of ideas or a pattern of imagery; it may include these but they are not its essence. The essence is a set of historical facts – with, we must add, an interpretation of them in faith. The faith is based on some things which have taken place in history; even things which are not happenings in history but which are eternal, like the existence of God, are known only in as much as they are implied by or revealed in these historical events. So, at least, it is commonly said. Primarily therefore the Bible is a supreme or unique witness to the saving events. The task of the scholar and theologian is not to meditate upon the patterns of the biblical text as it stands; rather, using the biblical text as a source, he presses towards something that *lies behind* the text. Because the Bible is an essential or sometimes unique source of information it can be regarded as authoritative.

This type of argument is very widespread and we shall spend some time in considering it from several points of view.

(*a*) This view seems to have the advantage of taking the weight of the revelation concept away from the Bible itself and trans-ferring it to the historical events regarded as revelatory. The action of God lies in the events – the exodus of Israel from Egypt, the life of Jesus, the resurrection of Jesus from the dead. The high status of the Bible does not come from its being an inspired book, given by God, but from its testimony to these events. It is not revelation but a record of revelatory acts, a testimony to them, a commentary on them.

(*b*) It would generally be agreed at the same time that the biblical data about the events are not necessarily historically reliable, at least when taken at their face value. There were indeed events, and these events are the milieu of revelation; but the biblical record does not necessarily, and does not in fact, report these events with complete precision and accuracy; or, to put it conversely, the events were not necessarily exactly as they are in the Bible. The status of the Bible rests on its giving testimony to historical events, but at the same time its record of these events is historically unreliable within certain limits.

(*c*) The biblical information about these events is never mere external or objective reporting, but is testimony in faith, a record of the events as seen through the screen of the faith which these same events generated. Just because it is a testimony in faith, it is natural that differing accounts of events should arise; these differ in their emphasis and structure, but are alike valid testimonies to the central event or events. The fact that, let us say, differing Gospels give irreconcilably different accounts of one event is by no means a negative factor; it rather confirms this approach to the status or authority of the Bible.

The sort of position adumbrated above is the one which has been preponderatingly used in the modern revival of the authority of the Bible. In the relation between event and interpretation, or in the notion of what the 'events' in question really were, there is room for much difference of opinion. The following is an example, using the story of Jesus' resurrection as an illustration.

(i) The majority opinion is that, in spite of the vagueness of relation between the events and the biblical reports, there was some external event, not entirely congruent with the description in the biblical text, but having some sort of recognizable relation with it – some reasonable analogy, or some imaginable path from the event as it took place to the event as it is reported. In our instance, there was some sort of real external event involving the physical body of Jesus and some process of 'giving life' or 'new creation'. The reports in the Gospels are various different faith-responses, which yield a testimony to the effect of the event on the disciples but do not provide good clues for the 'objective' reconstruction of the event, and indeed even suggest that it is quite wrong to seek any such reconstruction.

(ii) A moderately conservative or conservatively historical position would maintain not only that there was some such event but also that it can in fair measure be reconstructed from the biblical evidence. The Gospel stories do provide, within the recognized limits of this type of literature at that time, a basis for historical affirmations about the event; such affirmations not only can be made historically but also on theological grounds they should be made.

(iii) A more fully conservative position would go further in the same direction. It would suggest that the outlines of the event can be more or less directly read off from the biblical evidence, and that discrepancies between the various biblical sources, or between biblical sources and external evidence, can be more or less harmonized. For the resurrection story, it would follow the details of the text rather closely; while agreeing that the stories are theologically motivated, it would maintain that they are not *generated* by this theological motivation, and that on the contrary the theological motivation is a will-of-the-wisp unless the factual circumstantial character of the narratives be recognized.

(iv) At the other end of the scale, a much more 'liberal' or 'existentialist' position would maintain that the reference is indeed to an 'event', but that it is not an objective event in the outside world, but rather an event of faith in the experience of the believer. Thus the real event of the resurrection was the birth of faith in the hearts of the disciples, and all attempts to discover an external or objective content other than this are not only historically doomed to failure (since the stories were never intended as objective narratives) but also are theologically undesirable (since faith is not strengthened, but is actually destroyed, if one tries to support it by appealing to external events).

To sum up this point, then, it is clear that the emphasis upon events leaves us with a wide field of possible disagreement. Nevertheless it would be very widely agreed (a) that the Bible is of primary importance to us not through what it is in itself but through the saving events that lie behind it; (b) that the Bible is the principal, and sometimes even the only, source of information about these events; (c) that the biblical reports, for all their imperfections, have been generated through the impact of these events on men who responded to them in faith; the Bible is therefore not only a central information-source but a 'covenanted response', a response motivated by that very faith the generation of which was the purpose of the saving events; and (d) that there is some kind of analogy between the biblical presentation and the original event, sufficient to mean that the Bible mediates or communicates to us something of the essential shape or the salvific purpose of that original event.

If, then, this position has achieved such wide acceptance, is there anything wrong with it? What problems has it left unsolved? In what sense could it be said to be defective? There are several difficulties and uncertainties in it, but the main sense in which it is defective is the following: *it does not provide a conclusive and convincing reason why the Bible, i.e. just the group of books which constitute the present canon, should be 'normative' or 'authoritative' or should be the criterion of all our theological decisions*. In the eyes of those who doubt this account of the matter, this position can have seemed convincing only because most people were biased in favour of some kind of 'biblical authority' anyway. As soon as radical objections to such 'authority' are offered, it becomes plain, they maintain, that there is a great gap between the position which I have expounded and any decision about the function of the Bible in the present-day church.

(*a*) The idea of a series of 'saving events' itself contains a number of obscurities and possible contradictions. The subject is an enormous one and has been widely discussed; I shall leave it aside except in so far as it is necessary to do otherwise. For the moment it may suffice if I cite one expression of opinion contrary to the 'saving events' notion, from one writing within the present-day discussion of the status of the Bible. C. F. Evans writes:[2]

> The defect of the doctrine of 'salvation history' as presented in the writings of Oscar Cullmann is that it presupposes a kind of canal of sacred event or divine action flowing within the bounds of the world's history, with the consequent doubtful definitions and demarcations which go with determining where the canal is to be found.

Though this refers explicitly to Cullmann's ideas, it would probably affect most versions of the position which I have set out above. Now 'salvation history' is in Cullmann's own opinion the absolutely essential basis upon which the canon of the Bible, as the boundary of authoritative holy scripture, depends. It is dishonest in his opinion to claim for the Bible the status of holy

[2] *Is 'Holy Scripture' Christian?*, p. 59. On this in general see my own discussion in *Old and New in Interpretation*, especially pp. 65–102.

scripture unless it is based on salvation history.[3] The more emphatically the status of the Bible is made to depend on saving
events of this kind, the more it is damaged by any criticism of the
idea of such saving events.

(*b*) There is an important distinction between the 'authority' of a
historical source and the 'authority' of a theological norm or criterion. If we use the word 'authority', it means different things in
the two cases. There are events related in the Bible of which the
Bible is almost the only, sometimes absolutely the only, source of
evidence. For instance, there is extremely little information about
Jesus of Nazareth except in the New Testament, and the New
Testament documents come from quite near to the period of his
lifetime. This fact makes these documents the primary source for
his life and in that sense an 'authority'. This is true for most of the
historical writing in the Bible, for it is relatively seldom that a
biblical narrative is paralleled by an independent narrative of the
same events outside the Bible.

This fact seems at first sight to manifest the high status of the
Bible as the closest or earliest report of events. A moment's thought
however should reveal that this kind of priority as a historical
source is something different from theological normativeness. Even
granting that the New Testament is almost the sole independent
source of information about Jesus, this does not of itself mean that
our conceptions of God, or of ethics, or of the indissolubility or
otherwise of marriage, must be controlled by that New Testament
information.

This should be borne in mind for several reasons. First of all, the
principle is important that status as a historical source, or nearness
to the events reported, does not mean the same thing as theological
normativeness. Secondly, it is not the case that biblical reports are
always close to the events related. The latest New Testament documents are several times further away from the events than the
earliest such documents. In the Old Testament, some reports of
events in early history, such as the time of Abraham or Moses, may
be the best part of a thousand years from the actual events. The
principle of priority as a source, when applied rightly to the Bible,
will end up by making a very drastic division between the books
which have proximity to the events and those which do not.
Thirdly, though we have stated that biblical sources are commonly

[3] See Evans, ibid., p. 29, with quotations from Cullmann, and continuation of his argument on p. 30.

the major or the only sources for events related, this has to be qualified in two ways: (i) This is something that, at least theoretically, can alter; new documents can always be discovered which antedate those we now possess. (ii) This is itself in part a retrospective historical judgment, and not one which was at all times necessarily quite obvious. In about the third century AD, for instance, there were all sorts of documents in circulation which ostensibly narrated the life and teaching of Jesus, or the 'acts' of various apostles, other than the four Gospels and the Acts of our New Testament. To the naive reader, simply looking at all of these as they stood, it was not immediately obvious which had historical proximity to the events and which was derivative or secondary. Finally, books of a definitely derivative or secondary character sometimes found their way into the scripture. In the Old Testament Chronicles, though probably possessing some genuine old and independent tradition, is basically derivative from and inferior to Kings in its historical character, its originality consisting rather in the new theological colouring it gives to events, and the selection of them which it makes.

In general, then, the possession of proximity to the historical events is an ambiguous quality; and it does not of itself validate the status of the existing Bible as theological norm for today.

Another form of this same argument is to say that the Bible (or at least the New Testament, because this does not apply to most of the Old) comes from the 'first witnesses', the ones closest to the events in question, those who have been with Jesus himself and therefore would be likely to have the most genuine tradition of him, or alternatively, are witnesses of divine revelation at its culminating point. Factually, however, this is not particularly true; while some of the New Testament writings (some of the Pauline letters) come from an early time, they come from one who was not an actual witness of the acts of the pre-resurrection Jesus; some of the other New Testament writings are quite late, perhaps about a century after the crucifixion. The idea that the writings are holy scripture because they are 'apostolic' seems therefore to depend on legends, semantic misunderstandings and erroneous extensions of valid truths.[4]

(c) We return to some further questions about the 'saving events',

[4] See C. F. Evans' pages arguing that 'this image [i.e. the image that the New Testament was "apostolic"] is almost if not entirely fantasy', ibid., pp. 25–30.

and the relation between 'event and interpretation'. One of the ambiguities in this area can be usefully discussed if we make a distinction between three types of supposed 'event':

(i) There are events which in the Bible are ascribed to the action of God but which nevertheless are described as taking place under normal human and historical causation. Such are the capture of Jerusalem by Nebuchadnezzar (not exactly a 'saving' event, but by any account one in the series of major acts of God); the return of the exiles from Babylonia; the death of Jesus; the chain of circumstances which led Paul from Palestine to Rome.

(ii) There are events which would normally be regarded as 'miraculous': stories involving the splitting of the sea into a path with two walls of water on either side, involving a virgin birth, involving resurrection from the dead. I do not think I have to defend the use of the word 'miraculous' here; that is what these things are normally called.

(iii) There are 'events' which were not events at all. The story is complete legend and we recognize this fact. There was no flood that covered the world and wiped out all living things; there was no ark; there was no Jonah who fell into the sea and was swallowed by a fish. I do not have to argue this sort of thing; no one who is a serious participant in the discussion supposes that there were real 'events' behind these stories.[5]

Looking at the matter in gross, therefore, we have three categories, which we may call *immanent, transcendent* and non-events. I do not pretend that the distinction is water-tight; there are mixed and complicated cases: for instance, if you have normal human and historical causation, but influenced by communications from God in the form of dreams, angels and words of inspired prophets, to which class does that belong? Nevertheless our rough distinction will do for the present. The point has importance for the status of the Bible:

Those who have tried to vindicate the status of the Bible on the ground of the 'saving acts' which lie behind its narratives have often left it vague whether the acts belong to what I have called 'immanent' or 'transcendental' causation. The 'God who acts' type

---

[5] *Louvain 1971* seems to fail to face this obvious point; it solemnly discusses the varying relations between event and interpretation (see pp. 15f., 212) and does not mention the obvious and important case where there just is no event at all.

of theology made its mark precisely because it appeared to reassert the transcendental intervention of God in the world and at the same time to demonstrate a marked distinctiveness as against the environing religions. More recent works in the same tradition give the impression that there was no miraculous intervention but something more like a timely or providential concatenation of historical circumstances. The emphasis moves from external acts of God to *a kind of human thinking which operates in terms of acts of God*, and to the covenant pattern which is said to mirror them. But this covenant structure, which was supposed to be specifically Israelite and distinct from the surrounding mythological cultures, is now emphatically and joyfully derived from the Hittite treaties, so that after all the pattern is not distinctive, and at the most its application is. This would leave the impression that the transcendental causation, implied in the biblical narratives when taken at their surface value, is to be interpreted as real saving events, which are however of quite a different character, being in fact immanent historical processes. Where this is so, it is not unfair to say that the 'event' of the biblical narrative is a mythical representation of an actual saving event which is however of quite a different character. If this is so, then the term 'event' itself is becoming vague and equivocal.

This impression is strengthened when we add to this the 'events' described in the Bible which are in fact non-events. It means that the surface narration of an 'event' in the Bible in itself leaves us quite undecided what sort of event it is, or whether there is any real event at all. I do not maintain that this cannot be decided; I only point out that it is not decided by the fact that the supposed event is narrated in the Bible. The same ambiguity attaches to the assertion, often made, that Israelite or biblical thinking works in terms of historical acts. Does this mean that there *were* historical acts, *as* narrated by these men? Or does it mean that narration in historical-act form was their way of thinking?

What this adds up to is the following: the concept that the Bible depends for its status on 'saving events' is not nearly so far removed as has generally been believed from the function of the Bible as literature or as myth. We come full circle: the acts of God in their biblical form may end up by bringing us rather close to the world of myth and of fiction. Whatever the nature of the real events, it seems to be on *the telling of the story in this form* that the effective status of the Bible depends.[6]

(*d*) All talk of saving events as the basis for Scripture raises the question of why one must stop with the New Testament. Were there no saving events after the first hundred years or so of Christianity? This is of course a familiar question in all discussions of the status of the Bible; it involves its relations with post-biblical tradition, its relations with books which were in the course of time judged to be apocryphal, and so on, and I propose to discuss these under the topic of 'Limitation and Selection' at a later stage. I merely point out at this stage that, if the status of the Bible depends on saving events, the limitation of the Bible to books of certain periods produces problems for the idea of the events concerned. From the New Testament point of view, no doubt the most generally given answer is that Jesus is the culmination of the series of such events; there is, of course, salvation after his lifetime, but all thereafter is done on the basis of the complete work of salvation done in him. Whether this answer is satisfactory I leave aside here. It may be added however that a similar problem can be seen in the substantial time-gap between the main canonical Old Testament books and the New Testament. Where was saving history then? I have discussed this elsewhere, however, and will not pursue it at this point.[7]

(*e*) The real weakness of the attempt to base the status of the Bible on the saving events does not lie, however, in the ambiguity of the events themselves. It lies rather in the fact that the argument does not go far enough to bring us to the conclusion which it is usually supposed to demonstrate. It might demonstrate the authoritative status of some sort of creed, a list of major events with some interpretation attached. Interestingly enough, the time during which the argument from the saving events was stressed was also a time when it was popular to argue that many segments of the Bible

[6] Something like this is recognized and mentioned, though hardly accepted, by *Louvain 1971*, p. 15: 'Some were of the opinion that revelation was not bound to what actually happened in history but could even have taken place in the telling of the story (a minority in the British Group). But the great majority held that the historicity of the event is of decisive importance.'

[7] See my articles 'Le Judaïsme postbiblique et la théologie de l'Ancien Testament', *RThPh* (1968), 209–17, and 'Den teologiska värderingen av den efterbibliska judendomen', in *SEÅ* xxxii (1967), 69–78; also my Montefiore Lecture, 'Judaism – its Continuity with the Bible'.

had grown from primitive creeds or credal documents which were their nucleus. Moreover, the function of a *regula fidei* was carried out by creeds rather than by scriptures in wide areas of the ancient church. But what the argument from saving events does not demonstrate is that it leads finally, authoritatively and uniquely to our Bible, to the 66 books or whatever it is that we call by this name. Between the grounds of the argument and its conclusion there is a deep gap.

(i) There is a great deal in the Bible which cannot be classed as reportage of events, or not of the kind of central saving events which are a necessary foundation for faith, nor as interpretation of such events. It includes all sorts of historical, geographical, social, anthropological, legal and above all religious information. It includes ideas of God, views of the relation between man and woman, ethical norms, conceptions of the good life, notions of the meaning of death and of resurrection or immortality, views of the nature of man and the interrelation of body and soul; above all, it includes, whether articulately or implicitly, the various theologies of the writers. This last is really the point at issue. I believe that in the whole movement for the revival of biblical authority this was what was really sought: *that the theology or theologies of the Bible should be normative for all subsequent theology.* This is not an impossible position to maintain; but it is not at all demonstrated by pointing to the basic events which lie behind the Bible.

(ii) The argument might indeed have had adequate force if it could be shown that the theology (or theologies) of the Bible was entirely, exclusively and necessarily generated by the interpretation of particular antecedent events. But it seems clearly impossible to maintain this. To take the instance of the Pauline letters, let us accept that in a very general sense the ultimate purpose of everything written is the interpretation of the event of Christ. But the material used in the arguments, the cultural suppositions in which they are clothed, the general ideas about soul and body, about man and woman, about the law and the status of Jews and Gentiles – a great deal of this must be ascribed to a general cultural input. Similar arguments can be offered for any section of the Bible. And even where the theology of a writer can be shown to be entirely derived from the interpretation of events, the question still remains whether it is the *necessary* interpretation of them or only one among several possible.

In fact, a very large area of the existing Bible can simply *not* be reasonably regarded as 'interpretation' of antecedent 'events'.[8] At most, the event-interpretation schema can be applied to the main underlying theological skeleton. But this is just my point – the argument from events leads to some sort of skeleton or framework, or to a credal document; it does not lead to a Bible. I would myself, however, go further and say that even the main theological skeleton is only in part built upon the event-interpretation pattern; basic theological elements, like the basic Israelite idea of God, do not naturally fit this pattern.[9]

(iii) The view I am putting forward here, that those who argue for the status of the Bible on the ground of the saving events interpreted in it really go on to make the *theology* of the Bible normative, is confirmed by another fact: that throughout this period great emphasis was laid on the 'biblical way of thinking', the 'Hebrew way of thinking' and so on. It is natural to understand this as an attempt to make these ways of thinking normative for modern theology. This attempt itself provoked a certain amount of protest; Leonard Hodgson, quoted by Nineham, is typical:[10]

> It is, of course, true that the revelation given to us through the Bible comes through Hebrew minds, and that questions which troubled the Greek thinkers apparently never occurred to them. But to draw from this the conclusion that God wills us neither to raise these questions nor to seek to learn from those who have thought profoundly about them is ludicrously absurd. Why in order to be a good Christian should it be more important to have a Hebrew type of mind than to have a Hebrew cast of countenance?

[8] Naturally, any piece of literature can be somehow attached to some sort of event which occasioned it, even if it is a poet's walk over Westminster Bridge or indeed the event of his digestion giving him trouble one evening; but for our argument this is a trivial sense of the term 'event' and I assume the reader will not be misled by it. Within the biblical literature, of which much is history-writing, naturally thousands of events are recorded; but this again is something differing in quality, or potentially so, differing from 'revelatory events' in which God uniquely meets with man.

[9] For argumentation along this line see my *Old and New in Interpretation*, pp. 15–23, 77–82, and generally. Acceptance of these views is not however essential to my argument here.

[10] Hodgson, *For Faith and Freedom* I, p. 78; see Nineham in Hodgson, *Authority*, p. 94. Cf. also above, p. 49.

I shall not here be distracted by the question whether Hodgson is right in his protest against the giving of normative status to Hebrew thought. For the present we merely note that this sort of absolutization of biblical or Hebrew ways of thinking was in fact a feature of a powerful movement, rightly assessed as such by Hodgson. As I argue, a movement, which overtly sought to establish the normative status of the Bible on the ground of the events which lay behind it, in fact went much further than this argument could legitimately carry it and supposed that it had demonstrated the normative status of the thought-categories and theological methods of the Bible.

Some may still argue that it comes to the same thing. Hebrew thought does not work with abstract ideas but with historical events. But this is an obvious confusion. There is all the difference in the world between making normative (a) a set of events and the interpretations of them and (b) a mode of thinking which works in terms of historical events.

(iv) In this I do not argue that it was mistaken to go on and seek to establish the normativeness of the *theology* of the Bible; this was in many ways a right instinct, and one which fitted well with the whole movement for a 'biblical theology'. I argue only that the argument from events did not suffice for this purpose.

If so, we may ask, why was the insufficiency of the argument not observed? The answer must be, that those concerned were nearly all people who were in any case in favour of 'the authority of the Bible'; this is what they wanted anyway. Radical criticism of biblical authority, as we have it today, was then muted; it was widely agreed that a biblical revival was on the way and was to be welcomed; the task was more that of showing that such a revival was not a renewal of fundamentalist outlooks upon the Bible.

It is now time to sum up the results of our discussion in this chapter.

(*a*) The emphasis on the Bible as information about events seems at first sight very different from the emphasis upon it as myth or literature; but in the long run they appear to come closer together than was at first supposed.

(*b*) If the Bible is valued as information, it is really valued for information about the theologies of the biblical writers just as much as for information about events. The modern revival of biblical authority used very freely the argument from events, but its true interest was in the normativeness of the theology of the Bible.

(*c*) The argument from events does not sufficiently legitimize either the authority of the theology of the Bible or the uniquely normative status of *this* Bible as against some sort of creed or as against other interpretations, existing or theoretical, written or oral, of the same events.

VI

THE BIBLE IN THEOLOGY

It is, then, in the relations between the Bible and theology that the most crucial problems are to be found. In the history of theology, at least in Protestantism, this has surely been the traditional role of scripture: it acted as the final court of decision between the competing claims of different theologies. In the last chapter we suggested that the same was true of the modern reassertion of biblical authority: its real and primary interest was in making the theology of the Bible normative for the theology of today. The function of the Bible as norm for theology, or of the theology of the Bible as normative theology, is the real centre of the complex of questions which we are studying. In this chapter we shall analyse some of the initial problems in all this.

1. The Bible itself contains or implies theology. It would now be absurd to sustain the very traditional position that the Bible simply *is* theology, that each sentence of it is a doctrinal pronouncement, direct or indirect. As Vawter well states it,

> The traditional framework in which inspiration has been considered was erected around the concept that the Bible is a catalogue of doctrines, almost as a textbook of revelation, an earlier Denzinger whose every phrase was the statement of a dogma.[1]

The idea that the Bible is such a doctrinal textbook can be most simply characterized as a literary category mistake, obvious as such to any sophisticated literary taste but understandable as a result of

[1] *Biblical Inspiration*, p. 102. Denzinger, I should add for the information of the general reader, is the name of a Roman Catholic compendium of authoritative dogmatic decrees.

the way the Bible has been used over many centuries.

Equally, however, it would be a literary category mistake to suppose that the Bible contained no theology and that theology was a quite extraneous operation perpetrated upon the biblical text. Some have indeed suggested that the Bible presents something more like 'living religion' and that theology is a post-biblical phenomenon, constructing artificial structures on the basis of the written text. We can certainly agree that some elements within the Bible can be well characterized as 'religion' rather than as 'theology'; but this can hardly be carried to the point of denying the existence of theology within the Bible. In fact the majority of biblical scholars today are willing to talk of the 'theology' of St John, the 'theology' of the Deuteronomic school, and so on, and we should accept this as right.

A distinction has to be made however between *overt* theological statement and *implied* or *underlying* theology. Overt theological statement, in the form of considered and formulated doctrine, occupies only a fairly limited area in the Bible. Much larger areas are taken up by presentation in narrative form, poetic form, etc. It is perfectly proper to speak about the 'theology' of this narrative or poetic literature, thus the theology of St Mark, the theology of the P document, or the theology of a group of Psalms; but this theology is normally not overtly declared or formulated; it is conveyed indirectly through the selection and emphasis of material in historical narrative or poetic composition. Post-biblical theology, we may suggest, has been more concerned with the working out of overt theological decisions, with problems more expressly formulated; and in doing so it has tended to take as its central biblical base those areas within the Bible which also make their theological decisions most overt. The idea, now antiquated, that the Bible is a doctrinal textbook was an illegitimate extension of the overt theologizing of the Bible, to the point where all biblical expressions were regarded as overt theology; or, if not this, then as a sort of overt theology in disguise, which by application of a simple process (commonly an allegorizing process) could be converted into statements of overt doctrine. In modern circumstances, however, the identification and understanding of the implied or underlying theology of historical and poetical books has become a highly technical process, in which the theologian is largely dependent on the expert biblical scholar.

In general, then, and with the diversifications set out above, we should agree that the Bible contains theology and that there is thus a continuity between the theology carried on within the Bible and the theology of the post-biblical period.

2. We can look at this from another point of view by returning to our triangle of p. 61. Traditionally, theology was primarily a referential form of study. It sought to understand the entities like God and man, the events like creation and redemption. Its emphasis in using the biblical text was correspondingly referential: its interest lies in *that to which the text refers, that of which it speaks*. In modern times this point of view receives its most towering restatement in the Barthian theology. From the early stages, in the commentary on Romans, Barth was emphasizing that exegesis was not an understanding of Paul's mental condition, his ideas, his religious experience, but a comprehension of the *object* of his language, the object to which he bore witness; this is what I have called the object-centred principle of exegesis.[2] In general, it is probably still true that theologians, at least those of this and similar traditions, as distinct from biblical scholars, assign a primary place to some kind of referential understanding of language.[3]

In fact, however, the work of theologians is increasingly dependent on, and concerned with, the apex B of our triangle, the question of intention, the search for understanding of the mind of the writers. Only very rarely, as we now realize, can biblical passages be given direct referential interpretation; nearly always they can be used only in conjunction with the questions like 'What is the writer trying to do when he says this?' or 'In what connection does he use this expression?' or 'What was in his mind in the whole passage in which this occurs?' or 'What is the general point of view of the man who wrote these words?' and so on. This is in fact one of the great differences in modern theological practice: even when theology is very definitely based on the Bible, it does not proceed from biblical texts straight to the entities referred to; rather, it proceeds indirectly, and adumbrates its referential interpretation only *after* consideration of the mind and purpose of the writers.

This, in turn, is a main reason why the use of single sentences or individual proof-texts has died out; so long as a sentence was supposed to reflect an external entity in a direct referential sense,

[2] Cf. my *Old and New in Interpretation*, pp. 90f., 102, 182 n.
[3] Cf. my *Biblical Words for Time* (2nd edn.), pp. 197 n., 203.

such a use was understandable; now, since any sentence has to be correlated with others in order to see what the author may have had in mind, the brief scriptural quotation has ceased to be a demonstration of anything. The shift, we may remark incidentally, is accompanied by a change of meaning in English; when I was a boy a *text* was a phrase or brief sentence, learned up by heart because it was chock-full of good doctrine, or taken as the heading for a sermon; while today we use *text* for a full literary unit, a chapter at least or a complete book like Genesis or St Mark, *Hamlet* or *The Waste Land*.

The dependence of theology on the mind of the writers, as distinct from a direct referential understanding of language, has been made even more marked by the emphasis recently placed on the biblical thought-categories.[4] Sometimes one gains the impression that these thought-categories, or the biblical (or the Hebrew) way of thinking, are considered to be the primary normative aspect of the Bible for the theological questions of today. If this is so, it means a drastic shift of emphasis from the referential use of language to the mentality from which it issued, from point A of our triangle to point B. Whether it is desirable that such emphasis should be laid upon the thought-categories and mental systems of the Bible is another matter.[5]

3. From another side, the same relations can be restated as a linkage between theology and historical reconstruction. The referents of biblical passages are not only theological entities like God but historical events like the founding of Samaria, the finding of the law-book in the temple in Josiah's reign, or the journeys of St Paul. There was however an obvious relationship between the events reported in the biblical text and the possible purposes and motivations of the biblical writers, since the subject-matter overlapped. There is something in common between the historical narratives of Josiah's reign and the probable intentions of the Book of Deuteronomy, something in common between the historical reports about St Paul and the probable motivation of the writers of certain letters; there is something in common, but also, so long as traditional historical views are accepted uncritically, some element of conflict or contradiction. The process of bringing together these

---

[4] See above, pp. 3–6, 49, 86f., and again below, p. 164.
[5] See below, pp. 158f., 164, and my *Old and New in Interpretation*, especially pp. 34–64.

different kinds of evidence, and bringing them into contact with evidence from other sources, involved a work of historical reconstruction.

It was reconstruction because the historical account did not emerge straight from the surface statements of the Bible; an account other than, and differing from, these surface statements, but using them as evidence, had to be worked out. In particular, this meant that the real course of historical events differed at points from the reportage in the Bible, and that on the other side (at point B of our triangle) the persons who composed the books, and their ideas, motivations, intentions and theologies, were in some cases different from the surface statements of the Bible and/or from traditional views (for instance, of the authorship of books by this or that prophet or apostle) which had been taken as authoritative.

In saying this I am doing no more than to restate the familiar process of historical criticism in my own terms. I do this in order to bring out the connection between the rise of biblical criticism and the shift within theology from a more purely referential understanding to one much more involved in the purposes and mentality of the writers. It is in my opinion not so much a matter of theology accepting historical criticism or being influenced by historical criticism; I want rather to suggest a common shift of focus which affects both. This implication in a common intellectual standpoint means that the historical-critical approach should not be taken by theology to be merely preparatory or ancillary in character; on the contrary, it has essential links with the mode of working of the theological process itself.

4. Thus far we have spoken about certain relations between theology and the Bible. We have not, however, considered the question how far a theology must work from a biblical basis at all. Can there be a Christian theology which is not particularly biblical? Is there room for theologies which are more biblically-based, alongside of others which are less biblically-based?

This is certainly one of the key questions in the whole matter. The modern revival of biblical authority was in considerable measure, if not entirely, an attempt to exclude such entities as natural theology and philosophical theology from influence in the theological process. In Barth, for instance, natural theology was completely excluded; and if there was room for anything which might be called philosophical theology (I do not know if Barth uses the term, which is so far as I know an indigenous English term rather than a German one) its role would be an ancillary and clarifying one; it would not have an equal status with the dogmatic theology built upon scripture and certainly would not have the right to contribute insights of its own which might compete with or override the concerns of the other. In the 'biblical theology' period, though the sharpness of Barth's position was lacking, a hostility to the influence of philosophical questions and considerations in theology can easily be traced, and the excellence of the biblical way of thinking was often extolled precisely through the drawing of comparisons with the abstractness and unreality of philosophical thinking. This was a sign, perhaps, of a certain philistinism towards philosophy on the part of biblical scholars.

As has been pointed out above, however, philosophical theology has survived all this pressure and has in fact increased in importance and influence. It is doubtful whether anyone now wants to reduce to silence the voice of this segment of theology, and even more uncertain whether any reassertion of a biblical norm for theology could possibly do so. Though personally belonging to the biblical approach to things, and probably less inclined to listen to philosophy than I should be, I can no longer conceive that the status of the Bible in the church should be used so as to imply a denial of influence to philosophical considerations in theology; and I shall not treat the suggestion seriously hereafter.

Yet can we really suppose the problem to have been dealt with by such a declaration? Many will not be satisfied with it. The issue will be, for them, something like this: are theology and doctrine (and thereby preaching also) based upon something that we have received, that has been given to us; or do they in the last resort depend upon and consist of no more than our own ideas, however philosophically refined?[6] It is thus that the question will no doubt be phrased; and this still remains at the heart of all ideas of 'authority'. For philosophy, if it is to be taken seriously, has to have complete freedom.[7]

[6] Cf. below, pp. 129f.

[7] In saying this I do not necessarily admit that philosophical thoughts can be rightly characterized as 'our own ideas', as just something freely thought up out of our own heads. Perhaps theology has to regard philosophical thoughts as something 'that has been given to us' through the actuality of the world and of the human mind. But it does not seem necessary to pursue this further at present.

5. Perhaps however the conflict is not really so acute as this would suggest. We might consider the possibility that the difference concerns the *form* of a theology. Some theologies are very heavily exegetical; they incorporate large amounts of exegesis *in extenso* and give detailed consideration to biblical texts which appear to bear on the matter in hand at any time. Barth's theology is an obvious example. Another type of theology may avoid biblical and exegetical detail, and may concern itself rather with the statement of a general framework of belief. Tillich's theology contrasts well with Barth's in this respect. Is there an issue of principle here or not?

I would prefer to leave the matter open. It does not seem to me that, even granted the highest possible status for the Bible, it need follow that the *form* of a systematic theology must be highly biblical, or that considerable detailed exegesis must be incorporated within it; and it would seem possible that a more general and less exegetical form of theology would actually leave more freedom to the Bible, because it would provide a general framework within which the biblical scholar would handle the biblical material itself. This point is made, of course, independently of the respective merits and demerits of Barth's and Tillich's own products; we are speaking about the form of the theology in principle.

6. It can be maintained that a theology is not a mere explication of the biblical text, and that it cannot serve the Bible well if it seeks to be that. A theology, according to this view, is a statement in contemporary terms of what the faith of the church is. It is then not only permissible but essential that the theology should work with extra-biblical categories which are the categories of our own mental life. The theology would then have to provide space for its account of biblical elements which it considered essential; but its own structure, form and balance would not have to be derivable from the Bible.

Clearly, these questions about a more biblical and a less biblical form of theology produce endless new problems; and I propose to look at some other aspects before proceeding.

7. If the Bible is thought of as a norm, then there is a question at what point of the process the norm is applied. A norm may, for instance, be somewhat passive and negative in its application. The theology is free to grow in its own way and under a variety of in-

fluences, but at a final stage it has to submit itself to the norm of scripture. One often in fact hears the phrase 'final court of appeal' used of the Bible, and such a phrase presumably means something of this kind. This would recognize the fact that theologies have grown up in all sorts of ways and have historically used all kinds of categories and forms, biblical and unbiblical. No matter how they grow up, they have a final test of their validity to face. A test of this kind could well be mainly negative: it would judge that a theology had failed to provide for such and such elements in the Bible, and that it was therefore faulty. Such a test would not positively *direct* the incorporation of scripture in the construction of the theology. It would be somewhat like our criminal justice, which condemns us when we have committed crime but does not instruct us how to do right in the first place.

The norm of scripture could function in a much more positive and active way. It would be effective throughout the process, testing each element as it was thought out, dictating the order in which elements were to be taken, the categories in which they were to be expressed and the linkages between them.

I would imagine that where scripture was spoken of as the norm of doctrine the intention has usually been for the first, the more passive and negative, mode of operation; some, however, will almost certainly insist on the second mode.[8]

8. From the beginning we have observed that any modern idea of the status of the Bible appears to depend on the sort of hermeneutic process adopted. There is a hermeneutic relation between scripture and theology, and also between scripture and preaching; the theology is part of the interpretative process between scripture and preaching. All these relations are no doubt very complicated; let us concentrate on the relation between scripture and theology, and assume that what is said about it will be valid with suitable extensions for the others. In any case the problem is: if the impact of the Bible depends so much on the methods of interpretation, who decides which methods of interpretation are to be used? As we have suggested above,[9] if the methods of interpretation are so decisive, may it not mean that there are two authorities in the end, one of them the Bible and the other the interpretative method, or

[8] See the remarks about Luther's position in J. K. S. Reid, *Authority*, p. 60.

[9] See p. 8.

indeed that the final authority belongs to the interpretative method? This depends on the model adopted for the interpretative method, and three simple possibilities can be set out:

(*a*) First, a very positive model, according to which the Bible itself would dictate its own methods of interpretation. There would then be, so to speak, 'biblical' methods of interpreting the Bible. This is presumably what people mean when they talk about interpreting the Bible 'in its own terms'. This model can be commended both 'from above' and 'from below': 'from above' because it is a divinely-given authority, which therefore governs all human interpretation of itself; and 'from below' because any literary work has its own 'terms' (whatever that may mean) on which it should be taken and measured. Both arguments may be used together; but their basis is separate.

(*b*) Secondly, a much more negative model, according to which there would be complete freedom in interpretation but the biblical text would remain as a final instance. The interpreter is thus free to work in any way at all, but the biblical text remains as a solid fact, the source being interpreted, and it is thus the ultimate court of appeal against all alleged interpretations of itself.

(*c*) Thirdly, a model involving a high degree of interdependence; according to it the authoritative status of the Bible and the modes of its interpretation are intertwined, and one of them cannot be defined without a consideration of the variety of opinion possible in respect of the other.

In the first and third cases, any theology of the status of the Bible would have to include an account of the interpretative methods which it considered right.

9. In the modern discussion the special status of the Bible has often been linked with its *distinctiveness*: its ideas, its view of God and of the world, its picture of reality, are quite different from those presented by other religions and by their written documents. This argument is once again, of course, one based on the apex B of our triangle: it depends on assertions about the mentality, the world-picture, of the men of the Bible. No doubt it would go on to claim that this mentality is so entirely distinctive that it can only be explained as the impact upon these people of a quite distinctive transcendent act or acts. Even if the argument is extended in this way, the evidence appealed to still lies on the human, mental and observable level.

The argument looks at first sight like a strong one. The Bible does look very different, and even on the purely literary level, taking a literary-critical position with no theological axes to grind, one might be able to sustain this. Nevertheless it would seem unwise to depend too much on this argument, for the following reasons:

(*a*) The distinctiveness is at most only relative. In fact it is impossible to disguise the important elements in the Bible which are *not* culturally distinctive.[10] Even in the New Testament we have to leave room for the opinion that Christianity from the beginning was a syncretistic religion; even if one does not like this idea, it is a matter for historical research whether this is so or not, and it would seem fatal to tie the status of the Bible to a position which might have to be reversed with newer historical assessments. In the Old Testament, claims for distinctiveness of Israelite institutions and ideas can easily be overturned by future archaeological discovery.

(*b*) Claims for distinctiveness are really a matter for experts and go far beyond what theologians can control, much less the general clergy and laity. No one can know if something is distinctive unless he has read the comparable documents and sources. There is also an element of prejudice in this: in effect the place of the Bible is being supported by judgments which belong to comparative religion.[11] Comparative religion will very likely pronounce the Bible to have striking distinctivenesses, but will say the same thing about the other major religious traditions of the world. If all are distinctive, then distinctiveness does not really put the Bible into a special category.

(*c*) All claims of distinctiveness become again blurred when we look at the marginal literature, that which lies just inside the biblical canon or which came near to it but was in the end omitted.

10. Something must be said here about the relation between the Bible as a whole and the parts of the Bible. We have followed the general custom in speaking about the status or the authority of 'the Bible', but in fact for interpretation we can only handle a part at a time, or a few parts at a time; this is true, at least, for some levels of interpretation, if not for most. We may list some diverse assess-

---

[10] See my *Old and New in Interpretation*, pp. 34–64, for a fuller discussion of the argument from the distinctiveness of the Bible; and cf. again below, pp. 148f.

[11] Cf. again below, pp. 148f.

ments of these relations:

(*a*) Some have supposed that the Bible possessed authoritative status only when taken 'as a whole'. This would mean two things in practice: (i) that it was very important to attain global, comprehensive assessments of the Bible, and that these when attained would have very great value; (ii) that some elements in the Bible could be said to have little or no authority or even value in themselves, and to have such only when seen as part of the larger whole. This would be a typical 'biblical theology' viewpoint.

(*b*) A second position would accept that the individuality of particular passages was obscured if one always sought a pan-biblical comprehensiveness. The task, and especially the task of the preacher in trying to handle the exposition of a passage, was to work out the peculiar characteristics of *that* passage.[12] Would he then be wise to complement this with a balancing statement, pointing out that different viewpoints exist elsewhere in the Bible which thus relativize the position of his passage? Or should he let his passage have its own way, and leave it to be complemented at another time when he is talking about something else?

(*c*) Thirdly, it is possible to hold that the 'unity' of the Bible is not a principle of authority or a principle of interpretation, but rather something to be *sought*; not a starting-point but a goal of the process of study, interpretation and theological thinking.[13] If in fact the Bible in some sense comes from the one God, whether as inspired by him or given by him as authority, it would seem to follow that the end-product of its effect would have some sort of unity and not be absolutely self-contradictory. The questions would then be: is this unity something to be worked out theologically and *stated*, or is it something to be looked for in faith and hope? Does it mean one comprehensive unity, or does it mean a diversity of positions which nevertheless recognize one another as brothers, just as the divided branches of Christian faith recognize one another?

11. In this chapter we have concentrated on the use of the Bible in theology, but we have to consider the possibility that the major function of the Bible is not its part in theological thinking but its direct impact on the life of the Christian. For the distinction I am

[12] Cf. again below, pp. 175f.
[13] This view is (rather vaguely) suggested by *Louvain 1971*, p. 22 (para. 1); cf. below, p. 181.

indebted to the valuable article of David Kelsey.[14] He distinguishes two uses of scripture: in the first 'scripture bears directly on the religious life of the user of scripture', while 'the second is a more distinctively theological use of scripture because in it scripture bears directly on theological argument'. The second is the type to which most of our discussion has been devoted; let us consider the other in more detail. Kelsey writes of it:

> One of the marks of the man of faith is that he has found in scripture an illuminating suggestion about how to understand himself and his world. Theology consists of an analysis of this understanding of self and world. Scripture bears directly on the faithful man, helping shape his self-understanding. Faithful self-understanding, in turn, bears directly on theology, since it is the subject matter theology is to analyse and describe. Thus, by determining the Christian's self-understanding, scripture bears on theology, but only indirectly.

Kelsey cites as examples of this approach Bultmann[15] and John Hick.[16] Materially, these two differ very greatly; but 'the ways they relate scripture to theology are formally alike'.

Whether this is a correct understanding of the thinking of Bultmann or of John Hick does not concern us here; the distinction as pointed out by Kelsey is in any case an interesting one. What sort of judgment should we pass upon it?

The question obviously falls into two parts. Firstly, there is the question whether a 'religious' use of scripture, as described above in distinction from a 'theological' use, really exists and whether it is a good thing. Secondly, there is the question whether it is proper for theologians to base *their* conception of scripture upon this religious mode of its function rather than on the more strictly theological mode of its function.

The first of these questions must surely be answered in the affirmative. A 'religious' impact of scripture, falling directly upon the man of faith and offering him a mode of understanding for himself and his world, certainly exists; it is implicit in the reading of the Bible as literature, and in at least part of the use of it in

---

[14] 'Appeals to Scripture in Theology', *Journal of Religion* xlviii (1968), pp. 1–21; see pp. 2, 18–21.

[15] *Theology of the New Testament* II, pp. 237–41.

[16] *Faith and Knowledge*, pp. 127–32, 134–39, 196–98.

liturgy. Theology, with its careful formulation of questions and its search for answers to them, cannot hope to channel through its own procedures all of the impact of the Bible upon man, in its immeasurable detail and variety. Theological reflection tends to concentrate on certain key points, where present issues are to be seen; it has never distributed itself evenly over the entirety of the Bible. It is therefore very probable that much of the impact of the Bible falls upon man not through a directly theological reflection but through a more general 'religious' appreciation.

What is not so plain is that the Bible, thus appropriated religiously, is an entirely good thing. That one's understanding of world and self should be formed by the Bible means the provision of a context within which the basic decisions of faith and life can be made; it does not in itself guarantee that these decisions will be made rightly. In the purely religious influence of the Bible upon man there is, as seen from the viewpoint of Christian faith, an element of ambiguity. Such ambiguity does not need to be totally resolved; but in every generation there are ambiguities and issues which cannot be left to the uncriticized religious influence of scripture to control, and these it is the task of theology to disengage and identify, to conceptualize in the form of questions and to bring under the control of a disciplined discussion. There have been many examples of religious world-outlooks which have been founded upon the Bible, or supposedly so, but which have, in the judgment of Christians of other groups or of other times, appeared to be manifestly faulty. It is therefore necessary to examine such religious outlooks on self and world, in order to see whether their character really derives from the Bible or from some other cultural source, and to see whether their use of the Bible can be squared with the Bible itself, or with Christian faith itself.

If, then, a theology is an analysis of a religious self-understanding and understanding of the world, that understanding being influenced or even generated by the Bible but the Bible not entering directly into the work of theology, one must judge that such a theology is inadequate. To say this is not to underestimate what can be achieved by means of it, for we have acknowledged that such a religious (rather than theological) reception of the Bible plays a significant part; but such a theology would at least need to be supplemented by another approach, which would seek to *test* the current religious understanding of self and world by confrontation of it with the sources upon which it claims to draw.

12. There are many other distinctions which could be made between different modes of use of the Bible within theology. Indeed one can think of so many differences that it seems impossible to classify them completely, and I shall only list a number of ways in which one might slice the cake of biblical influence on theology:

(*a*) A distinction may be made between different *logical types* of use of the Bible in an argument. Kelsey, following Stephen Toulmin, distinguishes between *data, warrants* and *backing*.[17] In the instance offered, namely 'Harry was born in Bermuda, so, presumably, Harry is a British subject, since a man born in Bermuda will generally be a British subject', the *datum* is the fact that he was born in Bermuda, the *warrant* is the argument that people born in Bermuda are generally British subjects; if the warrant is challenged, it can be given *backing* in the form of statutes and legal provisions. The warrant must be general in form. The argument is of course a loose one and not logically coercive; Harry might turn out after all to be a Chinese subject. This lack of logical coerciveness might however be felt appropriate for the illustration of theological argument. What Kelsey finds (p. 17) is that 'In the arguments we examined, scripture was in fact almost always used as data, rarely as backing, and never as warrant'; the test cases were in Barth and Bultmann.

Following Kelsey's discussion, one wonders if the situation will not normally divide up as follows: the actual use of scripture in theology will normally be *data* in his terms; the *warrant* will be the general conviction that scripture has authority, is normative, is likely to be relevant, etc. (all of them *general* convictions about scripture, which fits with the analysis noted above); and the *backing* will be such arguments as can be found, let us say in a book like the present one, to sustain the validity of the warrant. But the three will be interlinked, because any form of backing will condition the way in which scripture may be used as data and any use as data will reflect upon the validity of the backing offered.

(*b*) The questions might also divide up along another axis, depending on the *practical context* in which they arise, thus:

(i) Theological questions in the stricter sense of the term, taking the form 'What do we believe?' Such questions arise from

[17] Kelsey, op. cit., p. 3 and generally; citation of S. Toulmin, *The Uses of Argument*, pp. 94–107.

faith itself, seeking understanding of itself.

(ii) Ethical questions, taking the form 'What is to be done?' or 'What is the right pattern of life?' It might be said that such questions arise from the world in which we live and are directed towards the faith by which we live.

(iii) Practical questions, taking the form 'How does the church express itself?' It might be a question whether these are really a separate category. I have in mind primarily the *form* of the church's speech, its exposition of the Bible, its preaching, its conversation with people and their opinions.

(*c*) Again, a distinction of *content* is often made within the Bible itself, for instance:[18]

(i) A distinction of status is often made between the truly religious or theological assertions of the Bible and those which seem to belong to other spheres. For example, it is common to say that the Bible does not claim or have 'authority as a scientific textbook'. This presumably means that its statements about cosmology, geography, the origin of language, and so on are of low status in comparison with the religious language of the Bible. Such distinctions seem helpful but their application in many cases is difficult. Could one also say that the biblical assertions about God had a higher status than those about the nature of man? If so, then biblical conceptions of soul and body, for instance, would have lower status. These conceptions however certainly border on the scientific. But in the Bible they are worked into the theological statements and cannot be easily disentangled from them.

(ii) A distinction could perhaps be made between subjects about which the men of the Bible 'really knew something', and things they really knew nothing about. This is a similar distinction to that outlined just above, but provides a different reason. The men of biblical times, it might be said, had no real knowledge of how the world began, of its remote geography, of the diversity and interrelationship of languages and peoples other than those of their most immediate environment; but they did have a real knowledge of some other things, such as the religious controversies of their times, the implications of the Israelite notion of

[18] I leave to a later point (see pp. 156–67) the more particular question of an 'inner canon' or principle of selection within the total biblical material. Here I consider more general distinctions, which are made or might be made, between different modes of function or validity of the Bible.

God, the tensions between Judaism and nascent Christianity, and so on. The content of the Bible would then be differentiated according to the degree of knowledge on the part of the writers (or the tradition behind them); where their knowledge was greatest, there would the value of the biblical material also be greatest, and vice versa.

(iii) A distinction is often made between the *general purport* of biblical passages and the *details* of them; the details, people often think, do not matter much, but a high status is attributed to the general sense of a passage.[19] Genesis 1, for instance, is often seen in this way. The difficulty, however, is that this is likely to lead to a conflict between vague assertions of what the passage means or of what 'the Bible says' and exact exegetical study. The latter may often show that the details were carefully thought out and deliberately intended and are essential for a grasp of the sense.

(iv) A distinction can be made between the *kerygma* of a passage, or its existential purport, on the one hand, and on the other hand the external data in which this purport is clothed. A related distinction can be made, following Bultmann, between *kerygmatic* statements and *theological* statements.[20] A phrase like 'Thy sins are forgiven' or, to cite Bultmann's own instance, the simplest sentence 'Jesus, Lord' (II Cor. 4. 5), would be kerygmatic; reflections upon them, or upon forgiveness or the being of Jesus, would be theological. Theological statements explicate the self-understanding evoked by kerygmatic statements. Thus the two function in different ways: theological statements are second-order statements and depend on prior kerygmatic statements. But, according to Bultmann, the two cannot be easily disentangled, for even the most clearly kerygmatic statements are already formulated in a theological terminology. Nevertheless the distinction remains one of paramount importance. Faith does not arise spontaneously out of human existence but is '*faith in the kerygma*, which tells of God's dealing in the man Jesus of Nazareth'. Theological thoughts on the other hand are 'the unfolding of the self-understanding awakened by the kerygma'. Though it is not easy or simple to distinguish between the two, it is nevertheless essential to do so, since it would be fatal if the status due to the kerygma were to be

[19] This distinction is further explored below, pp. 175ff.
[20] Bultmann, *Theology of the New Testament* II, pp. 239f.; cf. Kelsey, op. cit., p. 5.

attached to the theological thoughts.

This particular distinction has been expressed in highly special-ized Bultmannian terms, and it will not be further pursued in detail in this book. But it is not difficult to see that something somewhat similar exists in Anglo-Saxon thinking, even where Bultmann's influence has not been directly felt. People often feel that there is somewhere a core of material which is acutely personal, challenging and gripping; and that it is in this material that their faith is grounded, rather than in the totality of theological termino-logy in which the resultant thinking of the church is expressed.

It remains for us to bring this point of view into relation with the position expressed at the beginning of this chapter. There I sug-gested that, in the modern reassertion of biblical authority, the theology of the Bible was made normative for the theology of today. The position of Bultmannian type which I am now describ-ing may seem perhaps to differ from this and to make the kerygma normative for the theology of today, assigning only a secondary place to the theology of the Bible. Perhaps however the difference is only one at first sight. For Bultmann's object after all is to write a *theology* of the New Testament and he seems to consider this a task possible of fulfilment. His point seems to be rather that the theological thoughts of the New Testament can indeed be treated and understood, but *only* if they are understood to be secondary in relation to the kerygma, as explained above. Provided that the first-order place of the kerygma and the second-order place of the theological statements is properly understood, then a theology of the New Testament (and also perhaps, we may add, of the Bible, though that goes beyond Bultmann's own position) can indeed be, and should be, normative for the theology of today. The distinc-tion between kerygma and theological thinking is therefore not a real exception to the line of thinking expounded in this chapter.[21]

(v) A distinction may be made between what seems to come more directly from God (or from Jesus) and what is said about them, or said on their behalf by leaders of Israel or the church. For instance, many believe that sayings of Jesus are more directly authoritative than sayings of Paul. It may be replied that there are no direct sayings of Jesus, only sayings as reported by Mark, by Matthew, etc. This however is not the same point; we are not dis-

[21] Bultmann would, however, appear to exclude any theology of the New Testament built upon principles radically different from his own.

cussing the genuineness of the sayings ascribed to Jesus in the Gospels. Assuming that Jesus did some teaching, and supposing that we knew what it was, would it not have a first-order status while Paul's would have a second-order status?

This point deserves further elaboration, since several different questions are commonly mixed up here. We may analyse as follows:

(*a*) First of all, there is the historical question: how much is known of the genuine sayings of Jesus? About this, the opinions of scholars differ. In itself it is purely a question whether the information given in the sources is sufficient, and of the right kind, to decide the question.

(*b*) Going beyond this, however, there is a certain tendency to suppose that, if the exact words of Jesus could be recovered, these would, just because they are the genuine words of the Lord, possess a status superior to that of other sayings attributed to him, and superior to the things said about him by other writers such as Paul. We here pass from a purely historical question to a theological position, a position in which the exact and genuine words of Jesus take a notable priority. This position, we may add, could at least theoretically be held even if we remained uncertain what the exact and genuine words historically were.

(*c*) Against this we must however set a quite contrary theological opinion, to the effect that faith should not and must not be based on the historical accuracy of any genuine words of Jesus – this not so much because it is historically impossible to know these genuine words, but because such faith would not be real faith. According to this point of view, faith cannot be based upon such considerations as the mere historicity of the words believed in; this would be theologically dangerous and wrong. To support faith upon considerations of historical genuineness would, some would argue, be a contradiction of the principle of justification by faith. This last argument, indeed, is surely a perverse one: justification by faith was concerned with questions of obedience to the Law of Moses; its problem was with those who supported their faith with 'works of the law', not with those who supported their faith with a conviction of the historical truth of events or speeches related. Presumably the feeling is that faith must not be allowed to have *any* kind of support, and that support from historical genuineness is no different in essence from support afforded by 'works of the law'. In any case, whatever the merits of this argument, we here have a theological opinion strongly *opposed* to any priority for the genuine words of the Lord. According to this opinion, whether it is right or wrong, even if we do have some knowledge about the genuine and exact words of Jesus this is no more than interesting historical information; it would not be particularly decisive either for faith or for theology.

(*d*) My own position would lie between these two. One does not have to seek the exact and genuine words of Jesus as if these would provide the basic bedrock of faith in a way that no other written or spoken materials could do. On the contrary, one can accept that it may be impossible to identify any genuine sayings with certainty; and, even if any genuine ones can be identified, this does not of itself make them into the ultimate foundations of faith. Indeed, things said about Jesus by others might be equally central or even more central than his own teachings. This might be particularly so if we took the position that Jesus himself still stood within the framework of Israel rather than that of the church, and that the basic testimony to the risen Jesus comes from the post-resurrection church and not from within the teachings of Jesus himself.[22] All this being admitted, it seems on the other side perverse that out of theological zeal for the purity and autonomy of faith one should refuse to accord any kind of special place or significance at all to what can be known of the sayings and teachings of Jesus. And one cannot resist the feeling that some of the scepticism about the historicity of the sayings as reported in the Gospels is not genuine historical scepticism but a scepticism generated by the power of the theological will not to rely upon historicity as a foundation for faith.

(*e*) The question here is something different from what has usually been called 'the historical Jesus', that is, a Jesus explicable in immanent historical terms and thus one who differs from the object of faith and of theology. Rather, let us put it in this way: the Jesus who is the object of faith is one who lived in first-century Palestine. As a human being he presumably uttered *some* sayings; whether we know them accurately or not is another matter. Did his sayings represent a deep and serious understanding of the human condition? Christians surely believe, and must believe, that they did; if in fact his sayings were platitudes, inanities or rubbish, what effect would this have on his status as Lord? In this respect

[22] See again below, pp. 109, 167.

the status of Jesus is different from the status of those like Mark and Paul, who were interpreters of him. It seems a more serious matter to say that Jesus was 'plain wrong' than to say that Mark or Paul was 'plain wrong'.[23]

(*f*) This position does not contradict the view, commonly held, that the essential thing about Jesus was not his teaching but his person and the events which formed his ministry. This may well be true; but it should not be pressed so far as to suggest that salvation is focused in the *bodily* experience of Jesus, quite independently of anything he may have said or thought. A Jesus who contributed nothing through his thinking and his speaking is just as empty and unhuman a figure as a Jesus envisaged as a teacher of spiritual realities, independently of his bodily reality.

(*g*) The *originality* of the teaching of Jesus, however, is yet another matter. Many Christians have obviously been deeply shocked by the arguments of those who have tried to show, from the Dead Sea Scrolls and elsewhere, the existence of parallels to his teaching. The pain of this experience should have been unnecessary; it indicates a deficiency in people's understanding of Jesus and his relation to his environment. It is a cardinal error to suppose that the distinctiveness and honour which Christians accord to him as a person must be matched with an equal distinctiveness or originality in his teaching. Indeed, some of the adducing of parallels with the Dead Sea Scrolls has been cheap, malicious and sensational stuff. But the existence of parallels within Judaism, and especially sectarian Judaism, is nothing contrary to even traditional Christian doctrine; it should have been always known and acknowledged, and increasingly so with our increasing knowledge of the environment. Taken just as teaching, Jesus' teaching lay within the thought-world of the Israel of his time, and Christians should not have supposed otherwise. That which is peculiar lies rather in the linkage between his teaching and what happened to him.

(*h*) We began by considering that the sayings of Jesus might have more authority than those of Paul; and we here must add that some such distinction appears to be made by Paul himself. Forbidding divorce, he says that 'not I, but the Lord' so charges; concerning some other matters relating to husbands and wives, he says that 'I, not the Lord, say . . .' (I Cor. 7.10, 12). On another

[23] The phrase 'plain wrong' was cited already above, p. 42.

question he says that he has no instructions from the Lord, but gives his own judgment as one fit to be trusted (I Cor. 7.25). Note however that the distinction here is not between the teaching of Jesus and the teaching of Paul as totalities, but between one element and another within the teaching of Paul. Only occasionally (and in the earlier letters?) is the distinction drawn; and it leaves room for the view that the main body of Pauline teaching was regarded by its writer, except where qualified by this distinction, as having the higher, and not the lower, status of the two. Moreover, there is a question of whence Paul drew the knowledge that he called the commands or the words of 'the Lord'. It is not self-evident that they were actual sayings of the historical Jesus or written teachings such as are found in the present-day Gospels.[24] There are other possibilities, such as the thought of direct revelations made to Paul, or the utterances of Christian prophets within the church.[25] Thus in general, though the Pauline passages do establish a distinction between that which 'the Lord' commands and that which Paul commands, the distinction is a rather different one and has a different focus from that envisaged in any present-day discussion of the teaching of Jesus and the teaching of Paul.

(*i*) To sum up this point, therefore, many may think it reasonable to assign a first-order status to the sayings of Jesus and a second-order status to those of New Testament writers. But this does not necessarily mean a status of higher importance; I only point out some ways in which the distinction may perhaps legitimately be made or understood. One must at once admit that other factors can readily relativize it. Of these the most important which will be urged is the following: that the sayings of the New Testament writers take up a post-resurrection standpoint, from which alone the fullness of the meaning of Jesus, as Christians understand him, can be seen. This argument may be regarded as so overwhelming that other questions of first- and second-order status do not matter in comparison with it.

I started out in this chapter by saying that the most crucial problems lay in the relation between the Bible and theology. Since

[24] W. Kramer, *Christ, Lord, Son of God* (London: SCM Press, 1966), p. 160, says: 'For many reasons it is impossible to think that they could be actual sayings of the historical Jesus.'

[25] This is the view of W. Kramer, ibid.

no one now supposes that the true theology can be straight-forwardly read off from the pages of the Bible, any theological use of the Bible requires some distinctions of status, function and application. The latter part of the chapter has offered some examples of such distinctions; and the analysis offered is not an exhaustive one. I do not propose to work out the precise range and validity of all the distinctions which have been cited. I mention them in order to exemplify in a preliminary way the range and the complication of the relations which surround the whole subject. Of the points here touched upon, sufficient for our purpose has been said about some; others will reappear in our discussion later.

I conclude this chapter with a summary of the situation, which leans heavily on words of Professor Gordon D. Kaufman.[26] He has suggested that the traditional position of the Bible had three levels:

(i) First, the Bible was traditionally tied up with a whole view of the world as God's world; and through this it furnished a world-view, a total orientation for life.

(ii) Secondly, the Bible served as a resource-book, to which one could turn for guidance on all questions of truth, morality, etc.

(iii) Thirdly, the Bible was an authority for theology.

According to Kaufman, if I have understood him rightly, (ii) depends on (i) and (iii) depends on (ii). The first sense, however, has now departed: we no longer orientate ourselves to the world through a biblical framework. The framework through which we see the world is that furnished by science, by sociology and so on; what was once taken as God's truth is now seen as Hebrew or early Christian customs and folklore.

The loss of the first sense has caused a deep crisis in the second and third. The demand for biblical theologies, and other kindred approaches, and the whole modern reassertion of biblical authority, can be seen as a demand for authority on levels (ii) and (iii), after level (i) is known to have passed away. But in fact the attempt to reassert biblical authority in modern terms is a nostalgia for the good old days: the real question is the breakdown of the Bible as

[26] See his 'What shall we do with the Bible?', *Interpretation* xxv (1971), pp. 95–112. The thoughts which I adapt here come, however, not from that article but from a contribution to the discussion at Richmond, Virginia, in which all the articles of this number of *Interpretation* were discussed.

the fundamental orientation for western man. Whether or not we accept this analysis, it is worth pondering as one profound summary of the present situation.

The question that seems to emerge from this is the following: can anything *rational* be said about the status of the Bible in the church? Can an account be given of it which is honest both towards what Christians today believe and towards the world framework within which we live? The many clever distinctions and separations which have been registered in this chapter belong, I suggest, to an attempt to provide a rational account of this status, to explain why it is so and with what qualifications it operates. The alternatives to such a rational account would seem to be: either that we abandon the whole concept of any special status of the Bible and admit that it no longer matters very much; or that we continue to affirm for it the sort of special status that it used to have, but do so in an essentially irrational way, saying that it has for us this status but that we cannot really explain why. This chapter, then, together with those that preceded, has opened up for us the problems of a theological account of the status of the Bible; and in the next we shall try to adumbrate the beginnings of an answer.

VII

A BASIS FOR CONSTRUCTION

Can we then give an account of the status of the Bible within the Christian faith? On what principles shall we build such an account, and what purpose will it serve?

Perhaps the first thing is to say something of the atmosphere in which our undertaking is conceived. Here something of a paradox should be noted. On the one hand the question which we are discussing, the status of the Bible in the church and in Christian faith, is of quite paramount importance. It affects every aspect of the life of the churches and the presentation of their message to the world. My own position is in every respect in favour of a greater and freer use of the Bible by the church, and I believe that many of the troubles of modern Christianity are self-inflicted burdens which would be much lightened if the message of the Bible were more highly regarded. I have no faith in the vision of a Christianity which would emancipate itself more completely from biblical influence and go forward bravely, rejoicing in its own contemporary modernity. On the contrary, if there are resources for the liberation of the churches and their message, these resources lie to a considerable extent within the Bible. Present uncertainties about the status of the Bible, both on the sceptical and on the conservative side, make it more difficult to use these resources. Some of these uncertainties involve intellectual and informational confusions, which may be cleared up in part by the sort of analysis we have attempted here. Others are more existential conflicts, which are not to be removed by intellectual clarification alone but belong to the deeper struggles of the religious man with his God. All this is of vital importance: it is not a mere theoretical question, which might conceivably assist in dealing with the real problems; the question of the Bible is itself one of the real problems of Christian existence in the world.

All this on the one side; but on the other side I am not made anxious and unhappy by the fact that the status of the Bible is in question, nor do I feel any sense of pressure to vindicate its authority against sceptics or questioners. I fully expect that a very radical questioning of the use of the Bible in the churches will continue with us in the future, and I contemplate this prospect with equanimity. The reason for this lies in a shift in the locus of authority, or indeed an abandonment of the concept of authority altogether. The older theology seems to us today to have suffered from an authority neurosis; in all diversities there was an attempt to proceed from an agreed authority centre, defined and known in advance, which would serve as criterion in doubtful questions. If the authority was not clear, nothing could be done.

Today we are content to have criteria which are less clear, to leave the nature of authority to emerge at the end of the theological process rather than to be there in defined form at the beginning. Or, again, we might agree that there are different sorts of criteria, working at different levels and different stages. My own view is that no criterion is prescribed to a theology at its starting point; rather, any theology has to provide within itself, as part of its own account of its subject matter, an account of the criteria which it accepts, including its relation to the Bible; but it is only at the end of the process, as the final output of a theology is discernible, that it can be judged, and not by its relation to an antecedent criterion. I do not, therefore, suggest a chaotic theology which works with no criterion; criteria must be present and must in due course be isolated and revealed; but we are willing today to listen to the theology and consider its claims before we hear an account of its 'authority'.

For, to put it in another way, this book is predicated upon a multiplicity of theologies.[1] The older theological principle, if I do not misjudge it, did not think this way: rather, it set forth a criterion or authority which would, it was implied, generate the 'right' theology. No old-fashioned Calvinist, setting the Bible in the forefront of his theological programme, supposed for a moment that it might in the end demonstrate that the Pope was the Head of

[1] On this see Karl Rahner, 'Pluralism in Theology and the Unity of the Church's Profession of Faith', *Concilium* v (1969), part 6, pp. 49–58.

the Church. There was a strict line between the one authority and the one true theology; hence, exactly, the violence of strife between theologies which were closely related and accepted the one and same principle of authority. I am writing for an open theological situation, in the hope of providing something that may be useful for a variety of different types of theology. I leave it open therefore whether a theology will be of biblical form or not;[2] whether it admits 'natural theology' or not; whether its philosophical content is high or low.

Theological thinking today has an ecumenical setting; but the consequences of this have not yet been fully drawn. Those who are enthusiastic for the coming together of the divided churches have not always been equally catholic in their sympathy for divided theological opinion.[3]

Let us seek, therefore, to leave it open what the structure and principle of a theology may be. The only restriction I would specify is this: that if a theology is to be Christian, and not just theistic, it must do two things: (a) it must give some central place to Jesus of Nazareth; (b) its God must be the God who was already known in Israel. Perhaps it will be thought that this second requirement is not as important as the first, and that the inclusion of it is the special bias of my own theology. This I would admit; the relating of Christian theology to the Old Testament is of course my special emphasis and interest, and it does seem to me a more important question than any other question in the prolegomena of Christian theology. In any case, I do not think that in this emphasis on the God of Israel I put forward any sectional interest; at most, it is a highlighting of something that is generally held in any case.

It might indeed be held that this approach is a disadvantage and that one cannot think about the Bible realistically within the context of multiple possible theologies; that it would therefore be better to work out and state one theological position. The danger, I think, is this: that by leaving so many other aspects of the theological structure open one will produce too general, too formal,

[2] The distinction is exemplified from Barth and Tillich, above, p. 95.
[3] One reason for this is that the official or confessional position of churches is commonly much more conservative than the range of actual opinion within them; and enthusiasm for confessional reunion has been compatible with an intolerance towards the actual theological trends of the present day.

too abstract, and by consequence too legalistic a view of the function of scripture. Whether this is so or not, the risk is one I propose to run.

With these prolegomena in mind, we can proceed to a basic assertion like this: the status of the Bible is something implied in the structure of Christian (and of Jewish) faith. This seems to be the ultimate basis for all involvement with the Bible: it is a corollary of the faith, something implied by the basic constituents of faith. I do not say that, if anyone does not see this implication, or does not accept it, or even denies it, he does not have that faith; I only say that it remains nevertheless an implication of that faith.

Christian faith is faith structured upon a certain basic model of the understanding of God. The fundamental model was 'first worked out and decisively appropriated'[4] in the Old Testament. That model was reaffirmed, restated and reintegrated in Jesus. Christian faith is faith which relates itself to this classic model. The God in whom Christians believe is the God who was known in the Bible; the Jesus in whom they believe is the Jesus of the New Testament. This, I believe, would be, at least in general terms, agreed by most participants in the discussion.

This model was manifested, worked out, corrected and transmitted in the religious tradition of the people of God, that is, of Israel and later of the church. The tradition is human formulation, just as human in this respect as is the ongoing life of church or synagogue today, or indeed as the ongoing life of other human institutions which have some kind of tradition. It is a living tradition, containing all sorts of elements which in different ways mould the life of the people: stories of God's acts in the past, general historical memories, pieces of cosmology and geography, personal reminiscences, speeches of holy men and stories about them, lists and genealogies, hymns and folk-poetry, groups of observations on 'Wisdom', i.e. general matters of morality and manners. In order to meet new situations new interpretations of old traditions are given, and new traditions spring up; some old traditions die away, others are altered into new forms, others again remain as functionless survivals, which nobody knew what to do with but nobody took the trouble to eliminate.

Much of this tradition was at some stage oral; it was passed on by word of mouth, and was not written. On the other hand, some of it

[4] Words of G. D. Kaufman, *Interpretation* xxv (1971), p. 109.

was written from an early time. What was the development from this freer complex of tradition to a more closed body of written material, 'scripture'? This is a highly complicated and often controversial historical question, which could not possibly be analysed here. The motives and circumstances which occasioned the formation of a 'holy scripture' seem to be too various and too uncertain for any theological decision to be allowed to depend upon them.

What we *can* say something about is the effect of this change. First, it tended to *fix* the tradition in a distinct linguistic and literary form; this change, however, is not an absolute one, for written texts can still be altered, while some oral tradition is maintained in a remarkable degree of fixity. Nevertheless the alteration in general is as I have indicated. Secondly, it tended to reduce to oblivion all such tradition as did not attain to the status of scripture. By Hellenistic times the Jews knew extremely little of their ancient history except for what was registered in the Bible; and, similarly, extremely little of the early tradition of Jesus seems to have survived other than what is contained in the New Testament. Thirdly, the existence of a scripture did not stop the continuing formation of tradition; there now exist the written scripture and alongside of it the fresh tradition, and the problem of 'scripture and tradition' comes into being. Fourthly, the accepted 'scripture' is not the only book in existence. Other books are being written, and some of these may be considered as potential material for inclusion in holy scripture. The question which in the end came to be called the question of the canon of scripture had come into being.

There is of course no fixed point at which someone said that all existing valid religious tradition should now be written down, or at which someone decided that such and such written documents should uniquely have the status of 'holy scripture'. Our descriptions of these changes of status are mainly *ex post facto*, i.e. made on the basis of things as they are seen afterwards, after all the alterations have taken place. As has already been suggested, many of the acts and decisions which went into the process were very complicated; many of them were quite accidental in relation to the results which in effect emerged from them; and many of them can be known only by hypothesis, since direct evidence is lacking or is scanty. In the case of the Old Testament, it is agreed that the three great bodies of material, the Law, the Prophets and the Writings, came to clear recognition and definition in successive steps, the

Law being first, and that this corresponds also to a difference in degree of importance, the Law again being first in this respect (within Judaism; Christianity tended to value the various parts of the Old Testament more equally, and if anything to stress the prophetic element most highly). The total process lasted several centuries. In the New Testament the process did not take so long, but even so there was doubt and dispute about a number of books over several centuries.

Neither in the Old Testament nor in the New is there a sudden break which would separate the biblical period from the post-biblical. Of books of the same type written in the later stages of either Testament, some in the end were finally received as holy scripture, some were rejected, and some were received in some areas or groups but not in others. This overlap applies not only to books written but to the religious tendencies. The Old Testament in its later stages contains viewpoints which are characteristic of 'post-biblical' Judaism, and similar elements in the New Testament have features of 'post-apostolic' Christianity. Thus in general there is no sharp break and no complete separation between biblical and post-biblical stages of the religion in either the Old Testament or the New.

In spite of the slowness with which the outline of a 'scripture' crystallized, and in spite of the coexistence of scripture and un-written tradition, the existence of a scripture now creates a new situation. Both in Old and New Testaments the tradition, originally developing freely in a unidirectional manner, begins to curve back upon itself. The existence of a scripture has the effect of changing the character of the tradition; the tradition continues indeed to develop but now assumes to a large degree the character of an interpretation of the scripture; the scripture is regarded as having authority and appeals for justification are directed towards it.

This statement leaves all sorts of ends open, and we shall return later to talk about questions of canonicity and the like. For the present the main question is: what sort of status for the Bible is established by these observations about its origin?

The status of the Bible, it would appear, is established by two things: (i) the facticity of the decision to constitute it as scripture; (ii) the congruence of this facticity with the fundamental structure of the Christian faith.

(i) The fact that scripture was constituted as such, and separated

both from other written works and from the continuous accre-
tion of oral tradition, represents a fundamental decision to assign
a special status to the material it contains and to recognize it as the
classic model for the understanding of God. In a certain sense
therefore it is perfectly right to say that the Bible has this status for
us because these people, back in an earlier age of the synagogue and
of the church, decided that it should have such a status.

(ii) It would be wrong however to rely entirely on this rather
formal argument. It is not simply that the decision was taken in the
ancient church; it is rather that that decision makes sense in relation
to the basic nature of Christian faith. Faith is Christian because it
relates itself to classically-expressed models. This is much the same
as what people mean when they say, rather vaguely and ambiguously, that 'Christianity is a historical religion'. Christian faith is
not whatever a modern Christian may happen to believe, on any
grounds at all, but faith related to Jesus and to the God of Israel.
The centrality of the Bible is the recognition of the classic sources
for the expression of Jesus and of God.

The above is the fundamental position to be taken in this book;
but in itself it is not sufficiently clear until we add to it an inquiry
into some ramifications of the whole matter, as follows:

1. My argument has not at any point appealed to the literary or
religious excellence of the Bible, for I do not think this a satisfactory ground on which to base its status. This being said, there
is no reason why we should not recognize the outstanding literary
and religious quality of the main part at least of the biblical books.
There are some exceptions, whether in biblical books which fall
below the average of the Bible or in extra-biblical books which
come up to the level of the Bible; but in general the excellence of
the Bible in comparison with comparable literature would be
generally agreed.

2. My account of the matter, it will be noticed, is one framed
very much in *human* terms. It has not required any appeal to supernatural interventions, such as inspiration by God extending only
to certain books and no others, or the giving by God of the right
list of canonical books. The formation of tradition within ancient
Israel and the early church, the committing of the tradition to
writing, and the decision to collect a group of chosen books and
form a 'scripture', are all human decisions, decisions made by men
of faith but still human decisions and describable as such. There is

no special intervention here, but mental processes analogous to those which are found within the church of today. This is why they can be described in normal historical terms by biblical and patristic scholars; if descriptions are lacking, it is only because of lack of the necessary information, and not because there are elements transcending historical investigation. All this does not mean, however, that we have no use for terms such as *inspiration*; we shall return to it later.

3. If these are human decisions, are they then also fallible decisions? Undoubtedly. We have at no point said that everything in the Bible is right. That it contains statements erroneous in scientific and historical regards has already been implied above. But there is every reason to agree that theologically also the Bible is imperfect. It is not a textbook of the most refined Christian doctrine. I have based my position on its status as the classic model for the understanding of God, not on the idea that the model is a perfect one. The status of the Bible is one of sufficiency rather than of perfection. If I speak of imperfection, this is not in the sense that all human language about God must be imperfect; that is of course true, but we can go further and accept that theological statements about God which are more precise and correct than those of the Bible can be made and perhaps even have been made. Precision and correctness in theological statement is indeed not a goal which the men of the Bible always set themselves, nor one which they attained. But, again, it is not a matter primarily of intellectual goals or methods. The working out of the biblical model for the understanding of God was not an intellectual process so much as a personal conflict, in which men struggled with their God, and with each other about their God. It was, in Old Testament terms, a *rībh* or dispute, a controversy to which the public attention is drawn so that men can learn from it.[5] If there are distortions in the biblical picture of God, they belong not only to inadequate vision but to human resistance against God's truth and against insights seen by other men. The conflicts of traditions within the Bible reflect animosities and conflicts of emphasis between different circles of tradition, different writers. Later I shall say something

---

[5] This point of view is much used also by J. Wirsching, *Was ist schriftgemäß?* Cf. p. 229: 'This text . . . opens up a conversation space, in which the dispute between God and man, the battle over reality and the conditions it imposes on existence, is fought out.'

about how we can properly discuss the existence of theological deficiency in the Bible.

4. It may be noted that this position has been stated without any use of the concept *revelation*, which is commonly used in just this connection. I have avoided it on purpose because of difficulties and confusions to which it seems to lead.[6] For instance, one of the objections commonly raised against the special status of the Bible is the argument that revelation cannot be supposed to have ceased at the end of the biblical period. With my present form of argument, predicated rather upon the recognition of a classic model of understanding, the question does not arise. *Of course* God's people can be said to have received from him understanding additional to that which was available in the Bible. This does not alter the status of the Bible as the classic model for understanding.

5. But, it may be objected, is not the formation of the classic model just the same thing as revelation? And, if so, why should the completeness of the classic model have been reached at a certain stage? Is this not the same thing as revelation coming to a stop? No, it seems to me not to be the same thing. My account of the formation of the biblical tradition is an account of a *human* work. It is *man*'s statement of his beliefs, the events he has experienced, the stories he has been told, and so on. It has long been customary to align the Bible with concepts like Word of God, or revelation, and one effect of this has been to align the Bible with a movement *from God to man*.[7] It is man who developed the biblical tradition and man who decided when it might be suitably fixed and made canonical. If one wants to use the Word-of-God type of language, the proper term for the Bible would be Word of Israel, Word of some leading early Christians.

6. But then, it may be asked, are we not saying that the formation of the classic model is a human response to revelation? God has in the past done certain things which revealed himself, and the Bible is man's response to that revelation. This position is commonly held. But, if so, then why should one suppose that revelation, so understood, came to an end?

The common answer, no doubt, is that the final act of God in the series, the event of Christ, is a culmination and is the fullest possible

---

[6] This is argued more fully in my *Old and New in Interpretation*.

[7] I was already fumblingly thinking in this direction in my review of J. K. S. Reid in *SJT* xi (1958), pp. 86–93, and in *Old and New in Interpretation*.

revelation of God. Because it is in this sense culminative and final, one cannot speak of further 'revelation' which would add to it. Such new things as followed would not be additional revelation, but new acts of the risen Jesus who is the final revelation.

Is this a satisfactory position? Perhaps, if one insists on taking revelation as the initial point, and therefore plotting the scripture as a secondary point, a response to revelation, this is the best that can be done. But there are several difficulties in it.

One is that the sense in which Jesus is, for Christians, the revelation of God is very different from the sense in which any other event or phenomenon can be the revelation of God. Can such events or phenomena as elicited the Old Testament tradition really be called by the same name? Does the same not apply also to a host of minor events, phenomena and ideas which found their way into the eventual New Testament also? In sum, does not the sheer magnitude of the Christ-event within Christian belief tend, if the term *revelation* is used, to lead to the position that there was only one solitary real revelation in the full sense of the word?

Moreover, we have already called attention to the uncertainty about the status of the 'events', 'acts of God', and so on, which are supposed to lie behind the Old Testament narratives. In many cases it is quite uncertain whether external entities existed, or external events took place, in such a way as to form the 'revelation' to which the Old Testament was a 'response'. Jesus by contrast was an external phenomenon who existed in the world.

The real problem, as it seems to me, is that we have no access to, and no means of comprehending, a communication or revelation from God which is antecedent to the human tradition about him and which then goes on to generate that very tradition.[8] In attempting to found the status of scripture upon such an antecedent revelation we are explaining what is obscure by what is quite unknown. I am not saying that there was nothing there; only that (a) its status is too obscure for us to base anything upon, and (b) consideration of it thus becomes a speculative exercise in which we are not called to engage.

Would it be possible to suggest an alternative position? As I have pointed out before, the term *revelation* is not in the Bible a common general term for the source of man's knowledge of God, and some of the main cases found are eschatological, i.e. they look

[8] Cf. above, p. 17.

forward to a revealing of something *in the future*.[9] Perhaps this suggests another way of thinking. The main relation of revelation to the Bible is not that of an antecedent revelation, which generates the Bible as its response, but that of a revelation which *follows upon* the existent tradition, or, once it has reached the fixed and written stage, the existent scripture. The scripture provides the frames of reference within which new events have meaning and make sense.[10] The coming of Jesus made sense only because a frame of reference was provided by the existing Old Testament. The finality of Jesus would then mean not that 'revelation now ceases', but that the tradition of him in its classic and received form now becomes the framework within which events to come can be perceived and understood. This position would appear to avoid some of the difficulties inherent in traditional views; and it leads on naturally to the more 'future-directed' view of the Bible, to which further reference will be made below.[11]

7. But does the picture of the Bible which I am offering agree with the picture which the Bible itself presents? This question will certainly be put at this point. Does the Bible not present a picture of external divine acts and verbal communications from God? Is it not therefore, by its own account of itself, basically a communication from God to man, a 'record' of 'revelation'?

The answer to this is in two parts. Firstly, there is a difference between the surface account furnished by the Bible and *our* understanding of what was happening. Certainly, our classic model characteristically depicts a God working through external 'mighty acts' and speaking through direct verbal communication in human language; and this aspect, as we have seen, has historically had great influence on ideas about the nature of the Bible.[12] But though these aspects are prominent in the form of the model, they need not have the same directness when it comes to the effect of the model on our understanding. What I say is nothing new: in widely-accepted ideas of revelation, the aspect of verbal communication by God has already been greatly diminished in importance.[13] And

---

[9] See my article 'Revelation' in Hastings' *Dictionary of the Bible* (one-volume edition, 2nd edition, edd. F. C. Grant and H. H. Rowley, 1963), pp. 847–9; *Old and New in Interpretation*, p. 88 and *passim*.

[10] *Old and New in Interpretation*, pp. 19f.

[11] Cf. below, pp. 143f.   [12] See above, pp. 13, 76

[13] Cf. *Old and New in Interpretation*, pp. 16, 21–24, 77–81.

secondly, even in the surface form of the Bible, the reportage of divine communications to man is only one part; the form of many books is that of a man-to-man communication, of which many parts, but not all, report communications from God to man. The Pauline letters are letters from the apostle to the churches, not letters from God to St Paul.

8. This approach, I hope, enables us to bypass the opposition, which has now become a traditional commonplace, between propositional and personal revelation. The difference between the two has been endlessly emphasized in modern theology; in fact, as we now see it, the argument is not a very important one, and most versions of it confuse a number of different things.[14]

(*a*) The question of how God 'reveals himself', i.e. of how he communicates with man at all, is one thing; the question of the logical status of sentences in the Bible is another. Even if we insist that revelation is not propositional, this should not mean that we hesitate to recognize propositional material in the Bible for what it is. Conversely, the recognition of propositions in the Bible does not imply that these are revealed propositions or that revelation in general is propositional.

(*b*) The general position, according to which knowledge of persons and knowledge of truths, or belief in a person and belief in propositions, are two quite different kinds of thing, is itself a philosophical question, which I shall not try to argue out. It is at least possible that this is a false dichotomy: 'There is no antithesis between believing a proposition and believing a person if the proposition is taken to be the assertion of some person.'[15] Apart from the philosophical merits of the matter, it is observable that theologies which have emphasized a 'personal' view of revelation have in very many cases filled this out with a great deal of propositional content.

(*c*) In fact those who have opposed the 'propositional' understanding of revelation have commonly shifted their ground at points of difficulty by including some extra factor. For instance, they often begin by opposing a 'propositional' view and then go on to say that the Bible is not concerned with 'timeless truths'. But this is obviously a different matter. It would be the same matter

---

[14] In much of this I follow the recent article of Paul Helm, 'Revealed Propositions and Timeless Truths', *Religious Studies* viii (1972), pp. 127–36.

[15] Helm, ibid., pp. 135f.

only if all propositions consist only of assertions of timeless truths. Here again we find ourselves in the midst of philosophical complications, for it is a question what can be meant by a 'timeless' truth: does it mean (a) something that is true independent of all considerations of the time and circumstances of its origin; (b) something generally applicable, e.g. a saying like a proverb; (c) something elevated above all considerations of historical change and human vicissitude?[16] When people attack the propositional view, they seem to have in mind something like (c); but on any normal definition of what a proposition is, type (c) would form only a small proportion. If one turns to analyse what is said by theologians, it would seem that some of the things they say about God on the basis of the Bible are indeed timeless and are intended as such, in the sense that they are true at any time, e.g. the assertion that God is a living God; but, on the other hand, most of the things they say are in some way historically related – this however does not mean that they are not propositions, rather it means that they are *tensed* propositions.[17]

(*d*) Again, many of the arguments ostensibly directed against revelation through propositions change their ground and oppose revelation through *abstract* propositions. This is again a different matter, unless one so defines *proposition* as to include only abstract assertions. This in turn depends on what is meant by *abstract*. Probably what is commonly intended is not really abstract, but rather detached, neutral, objective information, demanding no response or commitment, and offering no personal involvement.[18] But this has now become something quite other than the question

[16] See Helm's analysis of some ways in which the notion of revealed propositions would entail that what is asserted is timeless or unhistorical, ibid., pp. 132–5.

[17] Helm, ibid., p. 135: 'Such assertions as "God was in Christ reconciling the world unto himself", which Christians confess to be a truth, were false when uttered before a certain date. This is simply to say that, being a historical religion, many of the crucial statements of Christianity are *tensed*.' On the logic of tenses, see especially the works of A. N. Prior, e.g. *Time and Modality* (Oxford: Clarendon Press, 1957); *Past, Present and Future* (Oxford: Clarendon Press, 1967).

[18] Helm, ibid., p. 133. Helm takes Bultmann, an extreme case, to be saying that 'if a sentence has a truth value, i.e. is an assertion, it is *ipso facto* an assertion of "timeless ideas" . . . and of matters that it is possible for the one to whom the assertion is made to regard detachedly or neutrally.'

whether utterances are propositions or not. As Helm puts it, the sentence 'There's a bull in that field' may conceivably be regarded neutrally, as pure factual information, but is more likely to be a warning, an expression of fear, a challenge to personal encounter with the bull, and so on. Conversely, if a sentence is to be 're-sponse-demanding', it must in very many cases have some truth value.

(*e*) What has been expressed as an issue about propositional revelation seems mostly to have been not an issue about proposi-tions (as against non-propositional communication) but one about the recognition of the *right function* of propositions (along with non-propositional verbal communications). Thus sometimes the question is of a kerygmatic or response-demanding function, as against a neutral information-giving one; sometimes it is a parabolic or indirect function, as against a direct one.[19] The issue here is a literary category-mistake, not a question whether the material is propositional or not. Failures to comprehend the literary genre lead to a use of the biblical assertions with a wrong function.

(*f*) It is often said that the conservative or fundamentalist view of revelation is a propositional one, and sometimes indeed this position is openly accepted by conservative apologists.[20] I think it likely that the real issue is rather that of genre and function.[21] Genre-mistakes cause the wrong kind of truth values to be attached to biblical sentences. Literary embellishments then come to be regarded as scientifically true assertions, kerygmatic words of grace and promise come to be taken as text-book doctrine. But, in so far as fundamentalist opinion takes biblical material as propositional in character, the proper response may be not to deny its proposi-tional character, but to say that, taken as propositions in the function supposed by fundamentalist opinion, the propositions are false ones. The long debate over propositional and non-proposi-tional revelation has at times been a circuitous evasion of this point.

[19] Cf. again below, p. 171.

[20] E.g. J. I. Packer, '*Fundamentalism' and the Word of God*, pp. 91–4. For a previous assessment by myself see *Old and New in Interpretation*, pp. 201ff.

[21] This is confirmed by the important part which the recognition of literary forms has played in making more flexible the doctrine of scripture in recent Roman Catholic discussion; see Vawter, *Biblical Inspiration*, *passim*.

(*g*) To sum up, then, the conflict between propositional and non-propositional communication, whatever its merits in a pure theory of revelation, does not appear to have important positive results when applied to the understanding of the Bible; and I shall not return to it in this book.

9. We now turn to the relation between scripture and the ongoing tradition. This is in many ways the most difficult part of the whole problem, and it is easy to fall into the traditional Catholic-Protestant antithesis which has so long been dominant in all problems of this kind. A common traditional Catholic position would say that the ongoing tradition complements and interprets the scripture; both alike are needed for the fullness of the church, and there cannot be a clash between them. A common traditional Protestant position would answer that tradition has the potential of going wrong and that if it did so it would by its exegetical function corrupt the message of scripture; tradition therefore does indeed have weight and importance, but exercises these rightly only if it is firmly placed underneath the prime authority of scripture. Is it possible to avoid this sort of antinomy?[22]

10. I am Protestant enough to think it clear that tradition can corrupt. I shall not argue the usual case for this, but shall make two other points which are not so often noticed. First, quite apart from the Protestant religious judgment, this judgment seems to be one which we as historians and biblical scholars are making all the time. We observe that in the course of time a tradition which has been received alters in the course of interpretation into something irreconcilably different. Indeed, it is not our place to make value judgments and say whether such changes constitute a 'corruption' or not; but we certainly do not, in our normal course of historical judgment, speak as if all historical developments of traditions were simply valid and natural extensions or interpretations. Secondly, there is no doubt that the relation of scripture and tradition is an annoying problem, which we would be glad to do without; but I cannot see that it is a *false* problem. On the basis of the Old Testament, apart from the New, the question is already set deep within Judaism; and it is repeatedly recognized as such in the New Testament, where it is basic to the ministry of Jesus and to parts of

---

[22] There is a flood of literature on this; but, among the items mentioned in my bibliography, see D. Ritschl, 'A Plea for the Maxim: Scripture *and* Tradition', *Interpretation* xxv (1971), 113–28.

the theology of Paul.[23] The position that the traditions of men can make ineffective the commandments of God is so pervasive there precisely because this was one major existential problem in all growth or change within a religion where a scripture already existed. Whether the Reformers were right or not in applying it to the late medieval church, it is certainly not surprising, in view of its prominence in the New Testament, that the formulation came to their mind. If one were to accept the New Testament picture of the matter and at the same time affirm the traditional view of an infallible Christian tradition guiding into the right meaning of the New Testament, so far as I can see that can be done only by saying that Jewish exegetical tradition was corrupting but Christian is not; but I would find this deeply offensive, and also quite unjustified by any scientific comparison of the methods or contents of the two processes.

11. We may enquire however whether the difficulty is diminished by our recognition that the scripture itself is not theologically perfect. This at least is an element which was lacking in the traditional controversy, for both Catholic and Protestant sides supposed that the theological teaching of the Bible was without error. If we now take a 'Protestant' position and hold that post-biblical tradition may err, we are at least not making the enormous qualitative distinction between an unerring scripture and an erring tradition. In both cases we are dealing not with a divinely perfect entity or institution dropped from heaven into the world of men, but with members of the people of God, sinful men yet reconciled with God, working in his service yet pulled in every direction by their own powerful convictions, convictions which are all the more powerful and all the more subtly distorting because these men are motivated not by love of money or of pleasure but by their will to do what is right and to express the will of God appropriately.

12. As we have seen, and as is now universally acknowledged, the Bible itself grew out of the tradition of Israel and of the early church. Tradition comes before scripture, as well as following after it. How can it be possible to restrict the influence of post-biblical tradition when the Bible itself grew up out of tradition? Here we have to give some thought to those who suggest that the creation

[23] On this see my arguments in *Old and New in Interpretation*, pp. 156–62 etc., and my two articles on post-biblical Jewish tradition in *RThPh* and *SEÅ*.

of a scripture was rather a bad thing,[24] and that we would really
have done better to continue on with oral tradition, restated generation by generation. At first sight this argument looks like an argument against the primacy of scripture: the formation of the Bible
was really a misfortune. But it can also be thought of as an argument against tradition. Once the scripture has been formed, whether
for good reasons or bad, it alters the position of everything else
within the people of God. Tradition before scripture is one stream
in which all theological thinking, all present-day influences, and all
historical memories are carried together; all are adjusted to meet the
demands of the new situations, and this is the present existential
decision of the people of God. The formation of scripture has the
effect of objectifying the classic model of understanding God; it is
now *there*, it becomes something to be looked at from outside,
something in which the new generations no longer participate in
the same sense, which is to them exterior and which they therefore
have to appropriate to themselves. The effect of this, I would
suggest, is to cause a deterioration in the character of tradition,
which easily becomes a mechanism for the manipulation of the
unchanging and objective scripture. The tradition is no longer the
total and existential life of the people of God; its range and depth
is limited by the existence in scripture of the objectified classic
model of understanding. This is part of the price paid for the
existence of a scripture. This price was nevertheless worth paying
because the classic model is itself a historic model, a fact of first
importance in the religious structure of Judaism and Christianity.
The model was fixed by scriptural form because it was believed to
be sufficient. If there had been absolutely no fixation, but only
endless rewriting and restatement, plus abandonment of the earlier
stages, this historicity would have been lost, in both of two senses:
first, the outlines of the model, in the form which they had in the
period of its working out, would have been lost through alteration;
secondly, the historical circumstantiality of that period, which is
incorporated into the form of the model, would also have seemed
less relevant and come to be abandoned.

13. There is certainly good reason to agree that the idea of
biblical authority can have bad effects on people. Given a wide-
ranging typological or allegorical interpretation, such as has been
practised during long ages of church history, the Bible can be

24 Cf. above, pp. 43f.

made to mean things quite opposed to the sense disclosed by a historical reading. A more literal and historical reading on the other hand can easily elicit a biblical legalism, which has been the curse of biblically-conservative Protestant streams such as Calvinism. Against this we must set the fact that legalism in one form or another is endemic to Christianity and is stimulated by many of the misunderstandings of it, not only by an excessive zeal for the Bible. If there is a biblical legalism where the status of the Bible is wrongly understood, there are also ecclesiastical and moral legalisms. There is, then, no question of suggesting that the acceptance of biblical authority has *uniquely* bad effects; we merely recognize that such bad effects do occur, just as bad effects can accrue from other emphases within Christianity. The fact that there is a fixed and objectively present canonical scripture can perhaps be a factor in inducing a fixedness in attitudes, in suggesting a finality and completeness in what is believed, in leading to something that is *a* faith rather than faith.[25] Such fixedness is not found only in association with Bible-centredness; but it is common enough in that association to force us to acknowledge the fact. A scriptural religion is not an unmixed blessing; it is foolish to ignore this, just as it is cheap and foolish to suggest, as 'progressive' people sometimes do, that Bible-centred attitudes are quite uniquely mischievous and harmful.

This takes us back to a point mentioned earlier,[26] and often cited in discussions about the Bible: the difference between 'our own ideas' and thoughts derived from the Bible. At first sight there seems to be a decisive difference here; but not too much weight can be placed upon it. It is often suggested that 'our own ideas', let us say our philosophical convictions, are our own property; the implication is that we have no right to inflict them on other people and that it is a kind of aggressiveness if we do so. Biblically-based thoughts, on the other hand, are supposed to come from beyond us; they are not our own property, they do not serve our purposes, and we in asserting them are not inflicting our self-assertiveness upon others. Against this opinion, however, we must judge that biblical ideas can and do very easily become 'our own ideas', and that this is just what happens with zealous biblicistic people. The fact that the ideas come originally from the Bible does not alter the fact that

[25] I owe this formulation to Professor C. F. Evans.
[26] Cf. above, p. 94.

they can come to be appropriated by people, who build their personalities around them, to the degree that they become very much their 'own ideas', with the accompanying moral implications. It is the same when people say that they are 'forced' by the Bible to believe so and so; often no real 'force' is involved, since such people *want* to believe the Bible, attach the highest value to believing it, and have made acceptance of it into their own first personal priority. But such things are just aspects of life with the Bible in the church, which have to be recognized and lived with.

14. We have to say something more about the element of error or distortion in the Bible. Doubtless the saying of this will provoke disturbance. To say anything like this is like poking a stick into a wasp's nest. It is the sort of thing people from television interviewers down (or up) fasten upon: *he said the Bible might be wrong!* The sad spectacle of people's concentration on one saying like this shows how largely the humanized and secularized man of today is imprisoned, in all matters concerning the Bible, within the categories of the fundamentalist approach. I am not asserting the validity of any cheap identification of theological error in the Bible, nor am I likely to admit that there is error in it at the points which the average man of today might be quick to identify as faulty, i.e. as not agreeing with what he thinks God should be like. I am asserting that the Bible has to be read critically; just as it has to be critically read in historical regards, so also it has to be critically read in theological respects. We read the Bible with a critical awareness just as we read Athanasius or Augustine with a critical awareness; and such a critical awareness is inhibited if we suppose that we have no right of judgment over the theological validity of what we read, but simply have to accept it because it is there. But the exercise of this critical faculty is a solemn affair, not to be undertaken lightly. And, in particular, it would be deplorable to think that one might simply identify passages containing error and thereby consider them as something to be ignored, while all other passages would be 'right'. This would still be a fundamentalism, applied selectively. If there is an element in the Bible of distortion of the ultimate truth about God, then that element does not attach uniquely to this passage or that but attaches to the Bible as a whole – though not necessarily equally over the extent of the whole.

15. With all this in mind we can conclude by returning to the subject of inspiration. It is clear that this would have nothing to

do with inerrancy or infallibility. It would have to apply in the first place not to the formation of scripture but to the formation of tradition in Israel and in the early church, the tradition which constituted the classic model for understanding; secondarily it would apply to the process of making this tradition into scripture, and thirdly but most unimportantly to the process of limitation within a sacred canon. The basic theological content belongs to the first stage, the formation of tradition. The real question therefore is something like the 'inspiration of tradition'.

Yet it is important to observe that the formation of tradition or the production of writings was partly incidental to the real vocation of leaders in Israel and in the church. A Moses, an Isaiah, or a Paul was not given as his main task the work of producing tradition or of writing parts of the Bible. Their actual task was one of leadership in the community of their own time; the production of tradition, and eventually of scripture, is, to use the technical word, a 'spin-off' from the actual work of leaders. The basic relationship was that of God with his servants, as his servants in their work in their own time. We are historically ignorant of much that they did or tried to do, and the scripture that remained behind to us easily bulks larger in our minds. In this respect historical scholarship has re-dressed a balance which within the Bible itself was already becoming wrongly weighted, and has enabled us to see such men as the prophets more fully as men who served God in their own time.[27] The status of the tradition incidentally produced by that service, and later that of the scripture itself, would seem to depend on the conviction that God was with his people in that service to their own time.

Can we say more about the *mode* of this, the mode in which God was 'with' his people? Here I am at a loss. Traditionally, I suppose, one would add 'in the Spirit'. Does this say anything more, does it make anything clearer? I confess I do not understand this well, but two thoughts may be offered to readers. First, 'the Spirit' in contexts of this kind seems to be used for a sort of linkage of meaning with presence. When human words about God are spoken, they have to be heard 'in the Spirit' in order to be rightly understood; not because the Spirit furnishes the intellectual links but because

[27] Cf. for the conception that the prophets ministered 'not for themselves, but unto us', I Peter 1.12, and my remarks in *Old and New in Interpretation*, p. 125.

when the words are understood they are accompanied by a mode of presence of the one of whom they speak. If this can be said of the understanding of scripture, it can perhaps be said also of the process of production of that same scripture. The relation of the biblical writers and traditionists to God through the Spirit is thus not basically other than that of the church today in its listening to God. There is however a difference in the *stage* at which things are: the biblical men had a pioneering role in the formulation of our classic model, and this may make it fitting for them to be called 'inspired' in a special sense.

The second point is this: in this exposition I have tried to avoid what is called a 'God-of-the-gaps' strategy, that is, an approach which explains everything possible on a human, historical and scientific level but then, at such points as show gaps in explanation at that level, suddenly ascribes the filling of the gap to the agency of God. If I understand rightly, the idea of the Spirit is of one who *accompanies* human thought and action; the human thought and action, however, can be given human and historical description, without resort to supernatural interventions at any points of difficulty. In giving an account of the nature of the Bible, this aspect appeals to me.

VIII

THEOLOGY AND INTERPRETATION

In order to be interpreted as a document of faith, the Bible has to be related to a theology. The Bible can probably be interpreted without a theology, but it would then be interpretation on a purely historical or literary level. The task of a theology is to guide, to inform and to discipline the affirmations of faith made by Christians.

The basic form of a theology lies in assertions of what is now believed by the church. Such assertions have to be fresh, that is to say, they have to be continually re-formed on the basis of critical reassessment. What is said now may well of course turn out to be identical with what was said before; but that will be on the ground of our decision now, our decision now that older assertions do not have to be altered. In this sense we may say that theological thinking is *constructive* in character: it is never simply derivative, never simply a restatement of a source. This applies also to the relation of a theology to the Bible. No matter how completely a theology may bind itself to a particular source or criterion like the Bible, its use of the Bible is still not a simple derivation and regurgitation of material from the Bible. A theological position must be more than a transcript of the Bible in modernized or in systematized form. It is not a historical description of what was believed and thought in an earlier age; it may indeed incorporate such earlier thoughts, but does so by deciding that these earlier thoughts can be appropriated and affirmed by us today.

1. A theology certainly does not draw only on the Bible as a source; it takes also into consideration a wide range of circumstances and realities, which we may perhaps generally designate as 'the situation'. Within the Bible on the other hand it has a task of selecting and ordering. This is true even of theologies which have seemed

highly 'biblical': their decision to be highly 'biblical' (perhaps, for instance, to deny any influence to natural theology) is itself influenced by what is discerned in the situation; and their task of selecting and ordering is just as great as in a less 'biblical' theology; perhaps indeed the magnitude of this task is the greater, the fuller the attention paid to the Bible. There are several circumstances about the Bible which encourage and require the sort of theological activity which I am describing:

(*a*) As we have seen, the Bible contains or implies theology, and this in turn provides continuity between the thought of the Bible and later theological thinking. Equally, however, the Bible falls short of being an explicit theological statement; much of its theology is implied and not overt. In order to interpret the Bible, a theology disengages a theological framework which seems to exist within the Bible; it makes this framework, much of which may be only implied, more overt; it makes the referential indications which in the biblical text are often lacking; and it integrates it into a statement of what is believed in the church of today. The constructive character of theology is determined by the unequal overtness and explicitness of the Bible itself.

(*b*) The same theological process is justified and required because of the *composite* character of the Bible, in which there is a great variety of time, culture, circumstance and viewpoint among the various authors and circles of tradition. In this respect it is unlike (say) the dialogues of Plato, which indeed also differ from one another and present differing viewpoints, but which at least are known (apart from pseudonymous dialogues) to go back to one single mind. The composite character of the Bible is an additional reason for the necessity of a selecting and ordering process in theology. In fact theologies noticeably do not spread their emphasis in a level way over the entire Bible, and tend to lay special stress on particular elements – often, ironically, elements the status of which within the Bible is rather precarious.[1]

(*c*) This process is also justified and required because of the *critical* nature of the use of the Bible in a theology, to which we have already referred. A theologically critical evaluation of biblical viewpoints can be carried out; but it cannot be legitimately carried out

[1] The classic example, I would think, is the amount of stress that has fallen in the history of theology on the birth of Jesus, an event which does not enjoy very profound rootage in the New Testament.

by cheap snap judgments against the biblical view. It can be legitimately carried out only in a full survey of all the evidence and in full consideration of the consequences for the totality of all theology. But with this reservation, and with the observation that the critical function of theology towards the Bible will normally be a selecting and ordering one rather than a plain rejection, we accept that the critical function is one of the reasons for the necessity of a theology in the interpretation of the Bible.

(*d*) The theological process is very likely to give profound attention to certain supplementary models furnished by classic periods of the early church; traditional christology and traditional trinitarianism are the obvious instances. Such models, while often lacking the historical and personal character and the literary circumstantiality of the biblical material, have a high degree of overtness and articulateness as doctrine.

In all these ways the theological process orders and selects the biblical material, while at the same time it relates the biblical material to extra-biblical realities, perhaps to philosophical considerations, to the experience of earlier theological work, and to the contemporary situation.

2. It may be asked whether within the framework of a scheme such as this there is room for anything that could be called a 'biblical theology', an 'Old Testament theology' or a 'New Testament theology'. My answer is that I do not consider this to be a question of principle, but rather one of convenience. The phrase 'biblical theology', it should be said, is here used in a slightly different sense from that in which I have used it at some points earlier in this book. What is meant here is something as follows: is there, between the exegetically describable contributions of particular biblical passages and the final theological decisions which are here outlined, some intermediate stage which would seek to state the theology of the Old Testament, of the New, or of the Bible as a whole? Profound works devoted to these subjects are, of course, already in existence. Yet their service seems to me to be in principle an ancillary one. In so far as it is a simply descriptive task, indeed, it may be found helpful to bring together the theological insights of the Old Testament or of the New, of the Bible as a whole. But room should also be left to the opinion of those who think that the texts are too diverse in their theological viewpoint for this to be usefully done. A *theology* in the full sense, one which takes the form

not of 'The Old Testament says *x*' or even 'the Bible says *x*' but of 'the church today affirms *x*' can never be attempted, much less carried out, except on the basis of *all* the sources and considerations which are relevant. The unity of theological thinking means that no issue of absolute principle is implied in the question of 'theologies' of parts of the Bible.[2]

3. As has been indicated, theologies can take many different forms. It does not seem that one can prescribe in advance for all cases the position which biblical material will take or the point at which it will be introduced. One would only say that a theology of primarily philosophical form would have to be prepared *at some point* to consider in what way it relates to the God of the Bible. Conversely, a theology of 'biblical' type, proceeding from ample biblical documentation, has to be prepared at some point to say how its thinking relates to extra-biblical considerations, of whatever kind.

4. We have been speaking of theology in the interpretation of the Bible for the church, and of the way in which biblical elements are used within the structure of the theology. But this does not exhaust the significance of the Bible for the church. The Bible cannot be properly interpreted without a theology, but the enunciation of a theology does not in itself constitute adequate interpretation of the Bible for the church. We have to consider also the homiletical task, that of expounding the Bible to the church. This brings us back to some of the same questions but in a different context.

Why does the Bible furnish the proper normal matter for sermons in church? In terms of our argument, the Bible furnishes the classic primitive model for the understanding of God, the model on the basis of which the church was founded and which itself was formed in the personal crisis of the church's beginnings. In its sermons, as in its liturgy and in the Eucharist, the church feeds anew upon that model.

But is there good reason why this preaching should have biblical exposition at its basis? Have we not admitted that more accurate theological ideas can conceivably be formulated than are found in the Bible? Should not the emphasis of preaching be upon what the church believes today? And can the Bible really be expected to answer the problems of people in the twentieth century at all? We are back with some of the questions which were posed at the begin-

[2] On biblical theology cf. further below, pp. 158ff.

ning of this book.

5. Although more accurate theological ideas can quite conceivably be formulated than those that are found in the Bible, this does not settle the question of preaching. The purpose of preaching is not to communicate the best theology. Though theology may be and often is more overt and more explicit as doctrine than anything in the Bible, this is not entirely an advantage; these qualities are gained at a certain sacrifice. In a way this brings us back, perhaps surprisingly, to the literary character of most of the Bible: its allusiveness, its circumstantiality, its many-sidedness;[3] all these make it fit to be the material upon which the church reflects and, if readers are willing to use the word *myth* in its most positive sense, to be understood as the basic foundation myth of Christianity – which qualities it has, as we have seen, precisely because it is in fact such a basic foundation myth.

6. Here we can go back also to our point about elements of error or distortion in the Bible. That such exist, at least potentially, has been admitted. This does not mean, however, that areas of the Bible can be dropped out of consideration as material for preaching on this ground. The problem of truth in the text expounded is something with which the expositor has quite normally to struggle as part of his task; it is not to be evaded by declassing any category of biblical material in advance, or by supposing some other category to be absolutely free from all possibility of such distortion. To say this is not to say that absolutely any passage of scripture must, simply because it is in the Bible, be suitable for choice as a text for preaching; there are other grounds on which passages may well be deemed unsuitable, but the question of theological error is one that has to be faced openly rather than avoided through silence.

7. But the question still insistently remains: why should one preach from the Bible? Why not just say what one believes to be true? The question falls into several parts:

(a) *Of course* one can preach other than on a biblical passage; one can talk about a patristic passage or a piece of modern literature, or simply say what one thinks about the task of the church for today. It is most important that one should have freedom in matters of this kind. But there is a difference between what one *may* do and what it is wise to do; between what one may do *occasionally*

---

[3] One might well cite also the *kerygmatic* quality of parts of the Bible, cf. above, p. 104.

and what one does as a rule; and between what is good for particular *individuals* and what is good for everybody to do. What is possible and permissible is not thereby also the most desirable course for the church in general to follow.

(*b*) One way of looking at the question, and one likely to be suitable in a tradition like the Anglican, is as follows: preaching is not just giving a talk; it is a talk in the context of divine service. But the liturgy is extremely full of biblical material, in prayers, readings, psalms, hymns and sacramental worship. One normal reason why preaching should be biblical is that, where there is so much biblical material about already, there should be some articulate interpretation of it. There is, we may suggest, nothing particularly Christian or particularly virtuous in the mere repetition of a great deal of biblical material in hymns, prayers and creeds, just because it is biblical. On the contrary, I have suggested that manifestations of a biblical religiosity may be something quite ambiguous.[4] The articulate interpretation of this biblical material is a way of sifting it, of relating it to what is in fact believable or believed, of giving it meaning in the present day. I would regard it as mischievous to assert that, because so much of the liturgy was biblical, the sermon could afford to neglect the Bible.

(*c*) But the argument is in any case valid only if one takes a conservative view of the liturgy.[5] The importance of the Bible for preaching can hardly be grounded on the biblical character of the liturgy, since liturgical reform might find it wise to make the liturgy less biblical. Whether such a step might be prudent I do not feel I can venture an opinion.

(*d*) It is of course excellent that one should also have the opportunity simply to state or to elaborate the faith as Christians believe it today, perhaps quite independently of reference to the Bible. As we have seen, such a course is very natural when one has in mind strangers to the Christian faith. Yet even then the basis of that which is said or believed must be just below the surface.

(*e*) In principle I find it very hard to lay down a definite rule about the use of the Bible as a basis for preaching, and I am not sure that it is the task of a writer on my present subject to do so. It would seem to me strange that I should predicate this book as a whole on the multiplicity of possible theologies and at the same

[4] Cf. pp. 101, 128f.
[5] Cf. above, p. 66.

time take it upon me to lay down the correct form and content for the task of preaching. For it seems clear that there are as many views and theories about the nature and purpose of preaching as there are theologies; but I personally am very ill informed about them, and find it difficult to go far into this area. It would seem to me dangerous if one, in working out a view of the status of the Bible within the church and its faith, were to think of legislating in the same breath about the form and content of homiletic practice today. To do so would certainly go beyond the competence of a biblical scholar; for, though there is a common homiletic *interest* within much of the biblical material and the life of the modern church, I doubt whether the Bible itself, even on the highest view of its status, furnishes models for the form and content of preaching which could be taken as normative.[6] I would think relevant also the distinction between preaching and teaching, between *kerygma* and *didache*: though the difference may often have been exaggerated, it would seem that there is something in it,[7] and that some of the task of biblical exposition, which would appear to emerge from the view of the Bible which I propose, might belong properly to the teaching function.

(*f*) We have agreed, then, that any emphasis on the status of the Bible cannot rightly go so far as to *forbid* any speaking in the church which is not expressly expository in character or which takes as basis the thoughts of some non-biblical writer. But two warnings, one more theological and one more practical, may profitably be given at this point. First of all, when one speaks on the basis of Kafka, or Camus, or D. H. Lawrence, or a newspaper article, one has a certain duty to make clear that this is *not* the church's tradition but something else; otherwise one runs the risk of a certain kind of Christian imperialism which tries to claim for Christianity everything that is wise and good.[8] And when one makes this honest disclaimer, one can then hardly, within the context of speech

---

[6] Cf. *Old and New in Interpretation*, pp. 144f., where I observe the virtual non-existence in the New Testament of the expository sermon as it could be thought of today.

[7] Cf. D. Ritschl, *A Theology of Proclamation* (Richmond, Virginia: John Knox Press, 1960), pp. 100f., and 97–103 generally.

[8] On this see D. Ritschl in *Interpretation* xxv (1971), p. 123, and his diagnosis of 'Constantinianism' or Christian imperialism in such movements as existentialist theology and the 'New Morality', *Memory and*

within the church, merely shrug one's shoulders at the question what the Christian tradition has to say, as if one could be indifferent to that; and since much or most of the Christian tradition has factually taken the Bible to be authoritative, one arrives back at the Bible anyway.

(*g*) Secondly, we have agreed that one may, rather than expound the Bible, 'simply state or elaborate the faith as Christians believe it today'. But in this there is a question of theological ability. Those who advocate such a course are often themselves capable theologians, with powers of original thought sufficiently developed to sustain the difficulty of what they propose. But the average clergyman would be well advised to develop his thinking through dependence upon, and use of, the basic documents of the Christian tradition, of which for homiletic purposes the Bible has always had priority. If a personal impression may be permitted, from one who generally occupies the pew rather than the pulpit: the quality of most preaching is shatteringly poor; and most of the laity would be greatly relieved to hear some talk, however simple in level, about biblical materials. The clergy often load upon themselves a dismaying burden in trying to produce 'relevant' and up-to-the-minute talks, which distort their calling and lie far beyond their competence.

8. This brings us however to the question of the relevance of the Bible to modern man. In what sense is it relevant, or how does it become relevant?

(*a*) In principle the Bible is an ancient book and no sleight of hand of interpretation will make it become anything else. Attempts to assure us that things in the Bible are 'exactly the same' as our situation of today are misguided. Paradoxically, it is only as we learn how different the Bible is, how far away from our normal experience (including our experience as twentieth-century Christians who read their Bibles!), that it can have its full effect on us. But the fact that a writing is old does not in itself constitute a major difficulty in its comprehension. Of the great literature of the world, the main part is 'old' – and continually becomes more so. Certainly, the fact that the Bible is ancient and classic literature means that it will not be appreciated without study and without

---

Hope (New York and London: Macmillan, 1967), e.g. pp. 135f. (existentialist theology), 182, 186ff. (the 'New Man' and the 'New Morality'), 192.

guidance from competent persons – which guidance today is amply available. Slick communication, providing 'instant relevance', is not a property of the Bible, and is not desirable in any case.

(*b*) More fundamentally, it must be doubted whether the main task of interpretation is to drag the texts out of their ancient setting and make them applicable to the modern world.[9] Rather, the Bible, the product of men in their situations in the past, feeds and illuminates the understanding of modern men in their modern situation. The Bible does not 'apply' directly to the modern situation, or commonly it does not; it builds and enriches the faith in which the modern man is able to see more clearly his own situation and judge his actions in it more properly. The relation between the man of the Bible with his situation and the man of today with his modern situation is provided by two things: that they are in the continuity of the one people of God and that their faith is related to the biblical model of understanding.

It is appropriate here to revert to the 'religious' use of scripture which Kelsey illustrated from Bultmann and John Hick and which he set in contrast with the theological use.[10] The latter is where the Bible operates in the course of theological argument; in the former, it operates upon the religious man, directly affecting his faith and his life. In this book I have spent much more time on the theological use of scripture, but we here see a place at which the religious use is probably very positive. For scripture to act as a *criterion*, a touchstone of decisions, it is in my opinion preferable to think of the theological use, which has the quality of explicitness and reflectiveness; but this should not be taken to mean that the other use does not exist or is not important. There is indeed some danger than any theological reflection about the use of scripture will, through a sort of theological professionalism, lay all the emphasis upon the modes of operation which are most overtly and explicitly

[9] Cf. D. Ritschl, *Interpretation* xxv (1971), p. 126: 'The traditional interest in "making relevant" the ancient words of the Bible or the church fathers to a present situation is not applicable. It is not the ancient words which are artificially transported into the present in order to become relevant, but it is the present occasion, the situation, which becomes transparent and relevant both to the ancient message and to the hope which permits the interest and concern for ancient texts. The starting point or place of beginning of meaningful theological reflection is in the present . . .'

[10] Cf. above, p. 100.

theological. This applies also somewhat to the next point, to which we now turn.

(*c*) Common ideas of the relevance of the Bible seem to go back to the old-fashioned use of it as a resource-book,[11] a work to which one could turn with one's problems and receive directions about what was right or what should be done. The idea that the Bible ought to work in this way is probably a survival of fundamentalism. I am not thinking only of crude and obvious matters, such as looking into the Bible to find guidance on whether women can wear trousers or go to church without a hat; I am thinking of the more sophisticated questions, often discussed in ecumenical gatherings, such as whether Christians should in certain circumstances support revolutionary movements, or whether they can offer insights which would help towards peace in an area of severe conflict. To me it seems not perhaps impossible, but certainly exceptional, that even a sophisticated consultation of the Bible can lead directly to decisions about such things. The Bible is not in fact a problem-solver. It seems to me normal that the biblical material bears upon the whole man, his total faith and life, and that out of that total faith and life *he* takes his decisions as a free agent.

(*d*) Even if we assign a high status to the Bible, this does not mean that we commence every process of thought within the Bible and laboriously struggle from that starting-point to arrive at a result effective in the twentieth century. The reader is at all stages within the modern world; his mind can range through the modern world and also through the ancient, in so far as he has sources and information. Knowledge of the past, even of the quite recent past, is almost entirely dependent on documents in writing; this is true, we may add, for a great deal of knowledge of the modern world, apart from what is most crudely present under our own noses. It is helpful to bear in mind that the personification of the Bible is only a figure of speech, and one which might best be avoided: the Bible does not *do* anything: it is read by people, studied by people, used by people in their arguments, interpreted by people. The people are people who are doing all this as part of the texture of their life today.

9. A point here touched upon deserves perhaps to be developed

---

[11] Cf. above, p. 110. At its worst, this use of the Bible can become an *oracular* one: one comes to the Bible with questions, which it is expected to *answer*.

more fully. The Bible is undoubtedly a document from the past, and this is equally true of other sources of theological models such as the Fathers, or the Reformers. This pastness of the ancient sources may be thought to have had an unfortunate effect, the effect of causing the church to locate its norms always in the past, giving room for the impression that 'God has since retired or withdrawn and that the theologians' task is now confined to the interpretation of what has always been true.'[12]

In general, we observe, the church has 'sought the criteria for her thoughts and actions in the past'. 'A review of the history of the search for and the discussions about *norms* in traditional theology would show that the church and in fact Israel in its later history shared with classical cultures an attitude of past-centredness.'[13] Certainly, it would be true of the twentieth-century revival of biblical authority, which took place more or less on a 'salvation-history' basis, that its effect was to tie authority more completely than ever before to a locus in the past.

As Dr Ritschl argues, however, the locus of decisions is in the present; and when the present is using past norms like the Bible or the Fathers it is using them as something filtered through the screen of a tradition in which they have been read. On the one hand, there is no direct access to an ancient source; it is perceived through the screen of more recent interpretation. On the other hand, this means that the sources are not in fact read as materials from an ancient world, suddenly dragged bodily into the modern.

Thus in Dr Ritschl's thinking the emphasis moves from that which was there in the beginning to a more future-directed picture: 'Scripture would be understood as the beginning of the ongoing tradition toward the fulfilment of Yahweh's promises.'[14]

A similar line of thought was included in the ecumenical study document:

Does the authority of the Bible rather consist in the expectation that the conversation thus established in the past will continue in the future? . . . God has spoken with his people in the past, and the fact of this past conversation is a promise that the conversation thus initiated will continue in the future. When God

[12] Ritschl, ibid., p. 122.
[13] Ritschl, ibid., p. 119. I am not sure how far it is justified to include classical cultures in the same category.
[14] Ritschl, ibid., p. 128. Cf. above, p. 122.

speaks for today, it is not through our taking the Bible directly and transferring its past utterances and their past meanings through barriers of time and culture change into the present day; it is rather through the promise which the Bible gives of a further, and similar, conversation.[15]

The present interest in the theology of hope and of the future is likely to stimulate further discussion along this line.

10. When we are talking about the emphasis upon hope and the future, it may well be expected that something should be said about the idea of 'progressive revelation', for this idea has been frequently used in the context of arguments about the interpretation of the Bible.

Everything depends on what is meant by the term. On the whole, one must say that the term was used primarily in the 'liberal' type of theology, to which, of course, the notion of progress was often congenial. Equally it was disliked by the more conservative spirit, and the 'biblical theology' movement also tended to dislike it. As expounded by a scholar like C. H. Dodd, who devoted a chapter to the subject,[16] its main point was that 'the work and influence of Jesus Christ' was 'the climax of that whole complex process which we have traced in the Bible', this process being 'of the highest spiritual worth', so that 'we must recognize it in the fullest sense as a revelation of God'.[17] With this was linked in his exposition a view that 'all increase in knowledge is in a real sense revelation'[18] and other views concerning the nature of genius and the self-unfolding of Reality, which I shall leave on one side. On the more purely biblical side, Dodd uses the concept to make a positive linkage of a kind between Jesus and the Israelite religious history which had gone before him in the Old Testament.

The same idea, however, was often used in a more negative way, as a means of dismissing substantial areas of the biblical material on the grounds that they stood at a backward stage in the great

[15] *Ecumenical Review* xxi (1969), pp. 147f. This line of thought does not seem to have been taken up in the final report, *Louvain 1971*. My own impression from the discussion was that this future-directed line of thought, though stimulating, was found to be difficult to pin down precisely, and in the event it was not very closely followed up.

[16] C. H. Dodd, *The Authority of the Bible*, ch. xiii, pp. 248–63.

[17] Ibid., p. 263.

[18] Ibid., p. 250.

progressive movement. Dodd himself mentions 'partly erroneous ideas of God, which are in time changed for ideas approximating more and more closely to the truth'.[19] Such an approach would have been disapproved by conservatives for its suggestion that there was error in the Bible in the first place; in the revival of biblical authority it would have been opposed both because this revival had a strong anti-evolutionistic aspect and because it sought, by seeing the Bible as a whole, to avoid the necessity for such gradations of value. Three points about the use of 'progressive revelation' in this respect can be made:

(*a*) The idea was used in order to downgrade elements in the Bible which were thought not to belong to its 'highest' points; the 'highest' points correspondingly received a great deal of attention. A good illustration is the high estimate commonly accorded to Deutero-Isaiah, a writer highly esteemed within liberal theology and considered to be the culmination of the prophetic movement, and even of the entire Old Testament.

(*b*) On the other hand the idea was used apologetically, in order to excuse and thereby justify the existence in the Bible of elements which now seemed discreditable. Such stories were 'primitive'; though present in scripture, they belonged to the earliest stage of its development and had been more or less negated or corrected by later emphases also within scripture.

(*c*) In either of these cases, whether the idea was employed in order to accuse or to excuse, its employment had a certain degree of condescension within it. But what more seriously damaged the notion of progressive revelation was its *inconsistency*. It was only by picking out a few favourite instances from the total history of biblical religion that a progression, in the form of an increasing approximation to ultimate truth, could be postulated. Those who used the argument of progressive revelation themselves usually considered large parts of the Bible to represent a deterioration, rather than an advance, on what had preceded.

(*d*) In all these ways the idea of progressive revelation must be considered to have been confused and unsuitable for the purposes for which it was used. Moreover, it depends on an idea of revelation which has suffered devastating criticism from more modern theological trends and which few informed theologians would maintain today. Nevertheless it may be possible to defend certain

[19] Dodd, op. cit., p. 249.

valid points which, no doubt, attracted some of the support that the notion of progressive revelation received. The dealings of God with man in the Bible are indeed describable as a cumulative process,[20] in which later elements do build upon what was said and done at an earlier time. As I have argued, the literature is meant to be read as a story with a beginning and a progression.[21] All 'acts of God' and incidents of the story make sense because a framework of meaning has already been created by previous acts, remembered in the tradition; they are 'further acts of one already known, of one with whom the fathers have already been in contact and have passed on the tradition of this contact'.[22]

All this can be argued without the unfortunate effects which have attached in the past to the idea of progressive revelation. What I now suggest does not involve an idea of revelation as a gradual dawning of ever purer light; it does not involve any evolutionistic notion of a progress towards something higher; and it does not involve any picking out of the high points in the Bible with a consequent downgrading of the remainder. It is of course perfectly true that one can find in various parts of the Bible elements which can be called primitive, in the sense that later biblical writers modified or even abandoned them; and there is no reason why this should not be said when appropriate. But it very often happens that such modifications, when the entire context is taken into account, involve just as much loss as gain. Thus the fact of progression within the biblical period and its literature can be properly noted as a fact for the interpreter and theologian, but does not mean that 'primitive' elements deserve any less attention or that 'higher' points deserve to be singled out for emphasis.

11. In conclusion to this chapter I shall add something that seems to make a tremendous difference to the atmosphere in which we approach all theological interpretation of the Bible. I refer to the concepts of orthodoxy and heresy. The question at issue is not what is orthodox, or what is heretical; it is rather whether we, in reading the Bible, have somewhere at the back of our minds the view that there *is* an orthodoxy and that the Bible will in the end express just that orthodoxy. Such an expectation would be in accord with traditional ways of reading the Bible. There is some-

---

[20] See on this my *Old and New in Interpretation*, e.g. p. 21.
[21] *Old and New in Interpretation*, p. 21.
[22] Ibid., p. 82.

where a narrow but distinct line of 'right opinion' or 'right doctrine', and all deviating opinion is heretical; the Bible is the ultimate mouthpiece of orthodoxy, and its voice will demonstrate that all substantially variant opinion is unorthodox. Use of the Bible is therefore undertaken with the discrimination between orthodox and heretical opinion in mind.[23]

As we see it today, however, this mental attitude is anachronistic. It sets forth, as the attitude within which the Bible is to be studied and as the goal of such studies, something that at the time was not there, something that is rather the product of later ages as they, in *their* situations of conflict and difficulty, used the Bible in order to form their decisions, and stated their decisions in terms which both used the Bible and drew hard-and-fast lines between the orthodox and the heretical. The biblical scene itself, by contrast, in both Old and New Testaments, is a vivid and lively pattern of argument and controversy; but though sides are taken very strongly, there is no picture of a fixed and standard orthodoxy to which the biblical writers uniformly conformed. Orthodoxy and heresy either were not there, or were not clearly marked and fixed entities.[24]

We can extend this in a further way. The sense which the reader derives from the Bible will depend not only on that which is positively stated by the Bible, but also on that with which the Bible is in conflict or, to be more precise, that with which the particular biblical tradition or writer now being read is in conflict.[25] The Bible contains not only its own theologies, but some indication of the anti-theologies against which they are worked out. Yet of these opposition viewpoints it may give only limited information; it may indeed fail to understand them properly.[26] Moreover, the

---

[23] This viewpoint is particularly marked in fundamentalism, where it can be regarded as really pathological.

[24] In this connection cf. the increasing influence of W. Bauer's *Orthodoxy and Heresy in Earliest Christianity*. Interest in this is marked by its recent appearance in English (London: SCM Press, 1972; German original, 1934); see the Appendix 2, 'The Reception of the Book', and among the English works mentioned cf. particularly H. E. W. Turner, *The Pattern of Christian Truth* (London: Mowbray, 1954), and A. A. T. Ehrhardt, 'Christianity before the Apostles' Creed', in *The Framework of the New Testament Stories* (Manchester: Manchester University Press, 1964).

[25] This point is formulated in the question (5)(c) of the study outline, *Ecumenical Review*, loc. cit., p. 148.

[26] For instance, the Old Testament frequently denounces the worship

reader here becomes dependent on a vast scholarly apparatus, furnished by studies in the Semitic and Hellenistic environment, by the history of religions, and by the researches into newly-found texts like those from Qumran and Nag Hammadi. For the normal student of the Bible, the scope and the technicality of all this study is frightening; yet if he does not allow his mind to be stretched by it, he then allows himself to be dominated by pictures of the religious opposition, if we may so call it, the anti-theologies of the Bible, which pictures are traditional and now archaic.

This in itself is perhaps an intellectual and pedagogic problem but it leads on to another of more direct theological importance. The religions of biblical times – Canaanite religion, Mesopotamian religion, Greek mystery cults, Gnosticism (if we count it as a religion on its own and date its origin far enough back) – did not merely furnish an opposition within the Bible, a series of anti-theologies. They also may have furnished – perhaps they probably did furnish – elements which had positive function within the Bible. How far this was or was not so is a question which I want to leave open; it certainly cannot be answered here, for lack of space and of knowledge, but that is not exactly the point. The point is not that it is difficult to answer but that no dogmatic or final answer can now ever be given. The degree of relationship may be great or may be slight; but we cannot assume any longer the picture of the Bible as the document of one religion, clearly demarcated against all others.[27] In this sense it is no longer a question whether the use of the Bible should become implicated in the general study of world religions; this has already become a fact, though the implications of it have not been generally drawn out.

Historically, the recognition of this problem is not new; it was already very much alive in the first decades of this century, with

of idols; but can it be said to have shown a real understanding of the deeper motivation for such worship? Did it understand the dynamics of polytheism? The understanding of polytheism which modern scholars have comes not directly from the Old Testament, but from Akkadian and Ugaritic texts and the like, used in integration with the Old Testament evidence. Cf. also above, pp. 97f.

[28] This among other things is the burden of J. M. Robinson's contribution to the Richmond discussion, 'The Dismantling and Reassembling of the Categories of New Testament Scholarship', *Interpretation* xxv (1971), pp. 63–77; cf. also his and H. Koester's *Trajectories through Early Christianity* (Philadelphia: Fortress Press, 1971).

interest in Mesopotamian religion and the mystery religions taking a lead in its formulation. The 'biblical theology' period tended, however, to minimize the importance of this material: emphasizing the inner lines of coherence within the Bible, it pictured the total shape of the Bible as something almost totally distinct from the surrounding world of religions. Such influences as these religions had were therefore only ancillary; they furnished forms and terms, which the Bible took over and shaped to its own ends as demanded by its own interior logic. Perhaps this is quite a good general picture of the situation; but if we are wise we shall build into our thinking an elasticity which will be able to accept, if need be, evidence of a much more positive part played by religions, opinions, and groups which later came to be regarded as idolatries, heresies and perpetual antagonists of the biblical faith.

IX

LIMITATION AND SELECTION

All modern discussions of the status of the Bible have to include a great deal of thought about two questions. One is the limitation of the Bible to certain books, when other books are not included within the Bible. This is commonly called the problem of the canon. The other is the principle of selection and ordering within the Bible, to which we have already referred. They can be designated as questions of external and internal selection: in one case, why are these books selected and others left out? and in the other case, why within these books should priority be given to this group of materials as against some other? The two questions indeed have much common ground and can in general be taken together. Both of them are problems for any one as soon as he abandons the most crassly supernaturalist view of the matter, i.e. the view that God inspired certain books and these only, and that everything in any one of them is of equal importance. Though the two questions have much in common, the external limitation of the Bible to certain books will be considered first; being a formal and external process with a clear quantitative element, its historical aspect is different.

1. *Formation and limitation of the biblical books*

As we saw above,[1] the biblical books, or most of them, began with a stage of oral tradition and reached written form later. Whether in oral or in written form, there was a process of restatement in the transmission; it involved compilation of differing sources, re-editing of the works in new form, loss of old sources which had been used but were no longer retained in their separate

---

[1] Cf. pp. 127f.

form, and reinterpretation of older elements within their newer literary context. In the Old Testament period some books may have reached their final form quite early; but others were then still only in their origins. In the Pentateuch, for instance, there were massive re-writings of older tradition in the stage of the Deuteronomic editing and again in the stage of the P editing (according to customary critical opinion, perhaps seventh and fifth centuries B C). The continuing interpretation of older traditions could take the form of re-editing an existing book, or again it could be done by simply adding on a new block of materials to one. Another way of up-dating an existing book was by rewriting the whole book from a new point of view. The books of Chronicles are a rewrite of Kings, and in this case both gained access to the canon of scripture, though in different sections: by the Jewish system Kings belongs to the Former Prophets and Chronicles to the Writings. The book of Jubilees is a rewrite of Genesis; but in the end it was not accepted as scripture except in certain remoter areas. There is in fact a continuous stream of production of tradition and literature, which really runs on to the present day, since there is no valid historical cut in it; from the Old Testament it is carried on in Judaism, from the New (and, after a gap, from the Old) in Christianity.

Of all this literature, a certain amount was put into some kind of special category, rather ill-defined, as holy and edifying material for reading in synagogue and church. If we start from the position of the average modern person, we have to strip away the picture of the situation with which we begin. There was no defined list of the canonical books until a late date, and it differed in different areas of Judaism, in different great churches. Moreover, as we look back at Judaism and the church, we tend to think of the communities which came to be regarded as 'orthodox', as the mainstream tradition. But in those early centuries it was by no means certain what was to be the future mainstream; there were many groups which diverged doctrinally, and such groups often shared some holy books with other groups but had some which particularly reflected their own doctrines.

From the point of view of the modern scholar we can perhaps best separate out, from all the totality of 'post-biblical'[2] Jewish and

---

[2] We have seen that this term is rather misleading, cf. p. 117; a good deal of literature commonly called 'post-biblical' or 'intertestamental' was written before the last Old Testament books.

Christian religious literature, those books which *in general literary genre* come rather close to the books of our Bible. This provides a sensible narrowing of the field. It would leave us, for Jewish books, with roughly the sort of books found in our so-called Apocrypha. Wisdom and Sirach certainly belong to the same literary genre as the biblical Wisdom books; Maccabees belongs roughly to the sacred-history genre, and so on. The books of our Apocrypha are Jewish books which were included in the Greek Bible but not in the Hebrew (though the original language of some of them was Hebrew); there are other such books, like the book of Jubilees or the book of Enoch, which also belonged to a genre approximately biblical and have survived in yet other lines of transmission (in the cases named, principally in the Ethiopic Bible).

Generally speaking, there are three lines of transmission for Jewish books, apart from those of the Hebrew biblical canon: (a) some books, though Jewish in origin, came to be abandoned by the main lines of Judaism, and were transmitted through their use by Christians: so for instance the Wisdom of Solomon, the book of Jubilees; (b) some books were never taken over by Christians and were preserved up to modern times by Jewish use: so for instance the tractates of the Mishna; (c) some books were not transmitted up to modern times at all, but after some time of use by Jewish groups, especially by sects, and possible influence on some Christians also, were lost and have been recovered only in modern times by archaeology.

What are sometimes called the New Testament Apocrypha are also in many cases works of literary genres similar to the New Testament – supposed Acts of this or that Apostle, Gospels, Apocalypses, Letters.

These last paragraphs are offered as guidance for the general reader who may need some orientation in the whole realm of apocryphal books and canon formation.[3] We can now proceed to the main issues that arise.

(*a*) It must be clear that there is a considerable amount of reli-

[3] The outstanding recent books on this which I have found are in German: H. von Campenhausen, *Die Entstehung der christlichen Bibel* (Tübingen: Mohr, 1968), and the collection of essays with critical discussion by E. Käsemann, *Das Neue Testament als Kanon* (Göttingen: Vandenhoeck and Ruprecht, 1970). Perhaps the most recent comparable study in English would be *The Cambridge History of the Bible*, Vols. I and II (Cambridge: CUP, 1970 and 1969).

gious common ground between the canonical books (our Bible) and other works which were similar and also contemporary. Just as we have already asserted that the Bible is not theologically perfect, so we have to add that the non-canonical books need not be theologically vicious. Distinctions of theological value may indeed be drawn, but these are relative rather than absolute; and they are not made on the abstract ground that this is found in a canonical book and that in an apocryphal book, but only after the same kind of sober and careful critical reading which applies to the critical use of the Bible itself. Thus, for example, a New Testament scholar in seeking to trace the important concept of the Son of Man is likely to turn alike to the canonical book of Daniel and to the book of Enoch, which in western churches is non-canonical; and he may well trace the New Testament usage back equally to both sources and find its background and understanding in both. In this sense biblical scholars in the course of their work pass quite normally to and fro across the boundaries of the biblical canon. This does not necessarily mean that they entirely ignore the boundary set by the canon; it is possible that, at least at one stage of their work, they may ask themselves not just what such and such a book means by itself but what it means that this book is part of the canon of scripture.[4] But even where this is done, the collection of relevant evidence and the preliminary assessments of meaning would already have included materials from within and without the present canon.

Readers will remember that my basic position about the Bible rested not on any completely decisive distinction in theological quality but on the facticity of the recognition of a scripture.[5] Those who in the ancient synagogue and the early church debated the limits of the canon doubtless used for their decisions various criteria, such as the supposed age of the document, the name of the writer, and the sort of doctrine it contained. The average modern scholar, I think, would say that there are marginal cases where the theological level of non-canonical books rises above that of elements in the canonical books of comparable period and genre, but that taken as a whole they do not approach, and certainly do not

[4] This last question is made into the main emphasis of biblical theology by Brevard S. Childs, *Biblical Theology in Crisis* (Philadelphia: Westminster Press, 1970).
[5] See above, p. 117.

exceed, the standard of the Bible. While we do not base ourselves on this argument, it would be thoughtless to ignore it.

(*b*) There is then a certain area of penumbra on the margin between scripture and non-canonical books. Only where conceptions from the older fundamentalism remain can one suppose that basic Christian decisions would be gravely altered if this book or that from the now Apocrypha were taken as fully canonical scripture, or if this book or that of the more marginal biblical elements were to be taken as outside the canon. Such changes would be of major gravity only if points of doctrine were established by single texts and if all individual elements of any work accepted were supposed to be equally and directly valid for the proof of theological positions – all of which, as we have seen, is no longer the case. It may indeed have been the case at the time in the past when decisions about canonicity were made; but it is not our position now. To give a personal opinion, I myself do not feel that if the Apocrypha of the present English Bible were considered to be fully canonical scripture it would make the slightest difference to doctrine as held by Christians today. Its main effect would be to add to the amount of material of which clergymen already complain that it is uninteresting, unreal and irrelevant to their flocks.

(*c*) Is the church then entitled to alter the canon of scripture? Undoubtedly. But a distinction should be made between two questions. One of them is a real and deliberate proposal to alter the canon. Someone thinks, let us say, that the book of Revelation should be dropped (some ancient churches were long without it) and the letters of Clement included (some ancient Bibles included them, e.g. the famous Codex Alexandrinus). Such a proposal can be made, and the church would have to discuss it, asking on what grounds the proposal was made; the grounds having been discussed, a decision would be taken. The suggestion is in fact quite hypothetical, and no such action is ever likely to be taken. Quite apart from the strength of opinion that there might be against any change of the canon, it is extremely unlikely that any one change in the canon would have better reason than any of five or ten others. This goes back to a point which has been fundamental to my thoughts on the whole matter: formation of scripture, and canonization of scripture, are processes which were characteristic of a certain time, a certain stage in the life of the people of God. We are in fact no longer in that stage; it is a matter of history to us, and even historically we are not too well informed of the arguments and categories which were employed – especially so, I would say, in the Jewish (as distinct from the Christian) process of scripture formation.

(*d*) The other question is commonly asked, characteristically, as a rhetorical question; it does not constitute a serious proposal to alter the canon. People say: Why can't one read St Augustine's *Confessions*, or *The Pilgrim's Progress*, instead of something in the present canonical books? Well, *of course* you can read the *Confessions* or *The Pilgrim's Progress*; indeed, you ought to do so. But what the question implies is not an alteration in the canon of scripture; rather, it is the abandonment of any definite scripture at all, and the replacement of what has been historically defined as scripture in the church by a selection from anything that may count as religious or edifying literature.

In other words, one must distinguish between the principle of a scripture and the merits of any particular list or canon of books. Proposals to alter the list are still proposals which presuppose a scripture. I have maintained that the existence of a scripture is built into Christian faith through its historical roots. The adoption of whatever may seem to be edifying religious literature is not a change in the canonical list but is a passing over to a different principle altogether.

Moreover, it is hardly necessary to point out that both the works cited in my example above were themselves second-order works in relation to the Bible, the *Confessions* at least in part and *The Pilgrim's Progress* in its entirety. That is, the writers considered their own work to have a derivative and secondary status in comparison with the Bible, to which they ascribed a relatively normative and primary status. This, moreover, is true of the vast majority of edifying religious books within the Christian tradition.

Our emphasis, be it noted, has lain on the formation of a scripture, which is something different from canonization, being both more important and much earlier in date. The definition of a canon is the marking of the exact boundary of scripture, the delimitation of it from other writings; it comes very late and is often specially concerned with those marginal writings the place of which is still disputed. Though explicit canonization comes late, this does not mean that the books attain only then to the status of holy scripture. The actual canon or list is a codifying, in a low-order fashion, of the principle that there is a holy scripture already fully recognized but with some degree of fuzziness at the edges hitherto.

Thus in general, to sum up this discussion of the external limitation of holy scripture, the whole matter is one full of historical contingency and relativity, full of elements which cannot be given a rational theological justification but which simply are there in their facticity. There is however also a practical aspect about the biblical canon, which deserves to be borne in mind: it provides a body of material of manageable size, showing (even if fortuitously) something of a reasonable balance between different genres, periods and points of view. The scholarly interpreter of it does not study it in isolation but in relation to a vast body of extra-canonical material, not only Christian documents later than the New Testament but also contemporary Jewish writings of all kinds and works from other religions altogether. I would, for example, consider the Mishna and Talmud to stand in valid and proper continuity with the later tendencies of the canonical Old Testament, and consider this relationship of Jewish tradition to the Bible to be of importance for Christian theological thinking also.[6] But that all the tradition which has validly grown out of scripture should therefore be canonized or thought suitable for the status of scripture itself seems to me from a practical point of view just fantastic.

The question of the canon, then, has much of the contingent about it; and at first sight it looks as if it offers serious difficulties to the status of the Bible as holy scripture. Such difficulties are in fact much more apparent than real in modern conditions. The problem of selecting and ordering within the biblical material is much more difficult, and has occupied much more of the attention of recent studies in interpretation.

2. *Selection and ordering within the biblical material*

We have already seen that all theological thinking involves some kind of selection and ordering within the Bible. It is now increasingly agreed that the Bible is not used and applied in a level way, but with the use of all sorts of priorities and preferences. What can be said about this process?

(*a*) First of all, it can be said that the process does not begin

[6] On this see my articles in *RThPh* and *SEÅ*, and my Montefiore Memorial Lecture 'Judaism – its Continuity with the Bible'.

through an antecedent judgment, made in abstract before the process of interpretation begins. The interpreter reads the Bible as filtered through the screen of the way in which he has been taught, or has become accustomed, to read the Bible. In other words, he reads it in a certain tradition, either an ecclesiastical tradition or an academic tradition, usually both. This earlier formation may incline the reader to go in the same direction; perhaps less commonly, it may drive him to go off in exactly the opposite direction – the same angle, but in the opposite sense. The problem of interpretation is not the problem of how one begins from the Bible without any previous understanding of what it should mean; the problem is rather how one is enabled to change from a previous interpretation to another one.

(*b*) Theologies and academic traditions make selections and give priorities within the Bible for reasons which have already been suggested. The Bible is not a unified writing but a composite body of literature. Even with a unified corpus of writing, let us say with the genuine writings of Plato, it is not easy and not desirable to attempt a huge and monolithic synthesis; even here the interpreter is compelled to disengage the lines and ideas which seem to him to be primary. The Bible is infinitely more disparate, in time, in place, in authorship and in point of view, than the works of Plato. But for the theologian more important still is the theological disparateness of the Bible: the degree to which the works are overt in their theology or implicit in their theology; the degree of their consistency within one work and in relation to other works; the degree of directness with which assertions of a part of the Bible can be applied to the external and referential truth claims which a theology must make. Thus the need for priorities and preferences is not only something imposed upon the Bible by ecclesiastical, theological and academic tradition; these traditions have imposed it because the biblical material itself invites and requires it.

(*c*) Granted therefore that such priorities and preferences exist, the question is how far they should be made overt and clarified, and how far they have to be controlled and limited. One of the features of a theology, as we have seen, is that its assertions about what is believed act as an interpretative structure to the Bible, picking out what seem to be essential points, the interrelation of which is likely to become the framework for selection and ordering of biblical texts by interpreters. Such a function has historically been exercised in particular by creeds and confessions; probably, I would surmise, the lengthier and more detailed confessions of the Reformation period, with the greater comprehensiveness of the matter they include, went further in this direction than the creeds of the earlier church. Except in extremely conservative circles, however, people would now be unwilling to think that these creeds and confessions, however worthy of respect, are the right hermeneutical keys and dispose the complexities of the Bible into a clear pattern of truth. In what other direction then may one turn?

(*d*) In one way the many-sided reality that was called 'biblical theology', and certain forms of Old or New Testament theology, were attempts to do this. I shall illustrate this from Old Testament theologies. Many of these, produced during the period about 1930 to 1960 which was (so far at least!), the great period for the subject, undertook to disengage a basic structure of the thought or the faith of the Old Testament, a structure which would take account of the different authors, historical periods and theological viewpoints but would show the essential interrelation of the concepts and mental patterns developed. The identification of this structure would enable the interpreter to distinguish between what was central and what was peripheral; the peripheral would be able to have meaning through the perception of its ancillary relation to the whole. It was certainly thought that the identification of the basic structure was something that must be done, and could be done, on the Old Testament's own terms – certainly not through dogmatic theological methods, and still less by application of the Nicene Creed or the Augsburg Confession. It was precisely for this reason that the movement called itself 'biblical theology': it was, or was intended to be, a mode of theology depending for its selecting and ordering work on the inner theology of the biblical books themselves.

Was it right or wrong in this? Is it really impossible to understand the Bible 'in its own terms'? Was it so foolish a dream that the Old or the New Testament should be able to reveal their own categories and structures of priority, and that these should be worked out by biblical scholars and passed on to the theologians for them to carry to a further stage? I shall not attempt to decide the question here. This aspect of the work of 'biblical theology' was left somewhat incomplete, and for a variety of reasons. Some said that the categories regarded as the Bible's own terms were just traditional categories of the old denominational theologies, Presbyterian or Lutheran or whatever it might be, imported unconsciously by the biblical scholars. Some scholars found a very different set of categories from those which others had found. Some thought that there should be a biblical theology, but that its aim should *not* be to reveal the structures of the Old and New Testaments. Others again were against biblical theology altogether. But in spite of the uncertainties which attached to the movement and the faulty work which was done under its banner, some solid results seem to have emerged from all the energetic work that was put into it. It is at least in principle possible that principles of structure and order may be identified from the Bible itself, or from major blocks within it; some such aspects are in fact, it would seem, very widely accepted, if also somewhat vaguely. The Bible is not an uncharted sea, a trackless chaos, to be mapped out only when the theologian[7] arrives with his compass, his sextant and his theodolite (a suggestive-looking word, indeed). In spite of some occasional cynicism from theologians, who tend to think that nothing makes sense unless theology is there, the Bible as seen from the point of view of the Assyriologist or the worker in Near Eastern Studies does not have a particularly chaotic aspect, and concepts for its interpretation can be disengaged just as they can for, let us say, the understanding of Islamic or Zoroastrian texts. Thus, to sum up, there is every reason to believe that studies on the lines of Old or New Testament theology will provide some preparatory mapping of the structures and stress lines within the Bible, and that theological work on selecting and ordering will have to take account of this. This is in fact now generally happening; I am not doing more than register something now already present but liable, since the misfortunes of biblical theology, to be ignored.

(*e*) What is most common in fact is the granting of a priority to certain parts of the Bible or to certain themes within the Bible. The place of election in traditional Calvinism, of justification by faith in traditional Lutheranism, are obvious illustrations of thematic priorities; and along with either of these tends to go a

---

[7] The reader will be aware that I use *theology* and *theologian* in two senses here. The form of biblical (or Old or New Testament) theology is: 'the structure of the biblical material is x'; that of theology in the strict sense is: 'the faith of the church is x'. I am sorry about this, but I did not invent the terminology.

certain concentration on the Pauline Epistles, with perhaps Galatians or Romans in the centre. A more cosmically oriented theology might emphasize the Johannine literature or Colossians. In extreme cases, not perhaps too seriously intended, such priorities have led to antipathy towards biblical books with contrary theological tendencies, like James or Hebrews. 'Liberal' theology in its heyday often showed a strong preference for the Synoptic Gospels or parts of them, and a corresponding downgrading of St Paul.

(*f*) Granting that such selection and ordering does take place, and that it is reasonable and necessary to some degree, what more can be said about it? Sometimes people speak of a 'canon within the canon'; but this seems to create an unfortunate impression, and I would use it only if giving a derogatory description of some one's mode of work. The word *canon* suggests something public, something ecclesiastically fixed, something formal and something list-like in character. Something similar can be said about the identification of a 'material centre' (from German *Sachmitte*). There is a certain difference between the two, in the following sense. A 'canon within the canon', an 'inner canon', an 'actual canon' in contrast with the 'formal canon'[8] – all such terms suggest a section of the Bible, a group of writings or a group of elements within writings, which take superior place. A term like 'material centre' may refer not so directly to a group of writings, but rather to a *central reality* to which they relate and which unites them. In this latter case the higher status belongs not to a part of the Bible, but to something lying behind the Bible which is the essential 'matter' of it. Examples would be the Resurrection or justification by faith, something which could be taken as a major theme and thus regarded as the organizing factor for all subsidiary elements. But the difference between the two cases is not an absolute one, for in the latter case scholars will nearly always have in mind some passage or group of passages which 'really' express and grasp this central matter; so that indirectly we are back again with a sort of inner canon.

Discussing these terms, *Louvain 1971* argues:[9]

True as it is that the interpretations contained in the Bible are not

[8] I quote the terms as used by K. Aland in his article in Käsemann, *Das Neue Testament als Kanon*, e.g. p. 155.
[9] *Louvain 1971*, p. 17.

all on the same level, terms like these suggest the possibility of establishing permanent distinctions. It is too easy to interpret terms like 'canon within the canon' and 'material centre' in a static sense. We cannot, therefore, attribute permanent authority to an inner circle of biblical writings or biblical statements and interpret the rest in terms of this inner circle.

What does this mean? In arguing against such a 'static' or 'permanent' position, *Louvain 1971* may be intending only to guard against the perpetuation of a wrong decision. Something may seem to us now to be central; later, in the light of further study, we see that it is not; but, if this had already received official recognition as the true 'centre' of the Bible, it would be all the more difficult to displace it from its position and put in its place what is now seen to be the true 'centre'. Some, however, might go further and hold that the actual centre will change with changing circumstances: in Luther's situation, they might say, justification by faith was indeed the true centre, but for our situation another centre has to be found. Thirdly, *Louvain 1971* may rather mean that any defining of a 'centre' in this sense should be resisted, and that all such identification should be on a tentative, temporary, and perhaps even personal basis only. With this last I would sympathize (see below).

(*g*) There is, however, in my judgment a more serious objection against any identification of an inner canon, a 'canon within the canon', or a 'material centre' as described above. The great danger of such distinctions is not that they lower other parts of scripture to an inferior status; it is rather that they tend to raise to too high a status the elements chosen to be central. These elements are then absolutized and regarded as beyond criticism. Against this I would urge that there is no element, whether we mean a portion of the Bible, or one of the events related by it, or a complex of theological entities believed in, which is so set above all others as to be exempt from critical weighing and measuring. Thus, in all ideas of an inner canon or centre within the Bible, the problem is not so much the use of this inner canon to measure the validity of the remainder, but the danger that this inner canon itself will be left unwisely exempt from theological criticism.

(*h*) In spite of these qualifications, it seems only right to recognize (again with *Louvain 1971*) that there are indeed some sort of nodal points (called *relational centres* at Louvain), such as the love of God or the resurrection of Christ, round which other statements are arranged and upon which they depend. Not everything, however, is decided even if these nodal points are identified; there is a difference according to the kind of matter involved. Some of the matter of theology is more fully biblical, some is less so. On the side of the matter which is biblical, in the sense of matter made explicit by the Bible, it is perhaps not difficult to agree which are nodal points in the Bible. Hardly anyone, surely, would doubt that the love of God or the resurrection of Christ were nodal points in the New Testament (for the Old Testament other nodal points would have to be found). But a theology may also have other nodal points for which there is only slight representation in the Bible: for example, the presence or absence of natural theology, or Tillich's method of correlation. Such theological problem-centres have a great effect on the ordering of biblical material, even though they are not represented in obvious nodal points of the biblical text.

In such matters the operation of selecting and ordering is part of the originality and creativity of a great theology; and there is no means of restricting and limiting the freedom of such decisions, nor would it be right to do so. In the modern theological scene these matters come not under the control of an authority which prescribes what is to be done and what is to be avoided, but under the criticism of a discussion which looks at what comes out of it. For such a discussion the essential prerequisites are freedom and the presence of adequate information: adequate personal contact with those holding contrary opinions, adequate means for the expression of these contrary opinions, and adequate means of circulation beyond the parochialism of particular groups of teachers or particular cultural streams.[10] One of the tasks of the ecumenical movement, and one of its achievements, is the provision of such a context for discussion.

(*j*) Modern historical criticism has introduced an additional dimension into the matter. At one time questions of selection and ordering were questions about the surface form of the biblical text,

[10] The discussions of biblical hermeneutics and authority repeatedly threw up the importance of the different national and cultural currents as a cause of differences within the universal church. The cultural parochialism of particular theological streams may come to appear as a more serious difficulty than their denominational affinities.

e.g. preferences between St Paul and St James. We now have choices between different layers, strata or editions of the same book. In a passage like the story of the Garden of Eden in Gen. 2–3, one can consider such stages as: (i) a possible pre-Israelite or pre-historic original tale; (ii) the story as an independent unit of Israelite folk tradition; (iii) the story as an element in the J narrative of the Pentateuch; (iv) the story as seen in combination with the P narrative in the final redaction of the Pentateuch; (v) the story as it was read and understood by men of the last stages of the Old Testament period.[11]

Because the story stands in each case within a different wider context, its meaning in each case is somewhat different. The question might then be asked, which of these stages is the decisive one for the theological interpreter? The question is answered as soon as it is formulated. The idea that only one stage out of these different historical stages should become theologically decisive is denied by everything that we have said. In principle the interpreter is entitled to take as the text for interpretation any of the stages which can be identified or all of them; the only one which might have to be excepted is, in the case of story and legend elements which have been adopted from a quite pagan and non-Israelite origin, the meaning in that pre-Israelite stage; this stage, which might be polytheistic, would be *relevant* for explanation, but would not in itself be a stage in the experience and tradition of Israel as such.

But though in principle all stages of the tradition which went to make up scripture are relevant, a certain basic character attaches to the text of the literary units as they now are. Purely practically, this is in most cases the one stage which is objectively available to us; all others are a matter of historical reconstruction, however probable. From the point of view of modern literary appreciation,

[11] One could extend this without limit, by asking how the story was read in the third century AD, in the tenth, in the nineteenth, and so on. This extension is legitimate but to some extent is a different matter from what I here have in mind. I am here concerned with the strata as they may be distinguished within the total period of creation and crystallization of the Old Testament itself. The evidence for these strata is evidence within the Old Testament text. In asking how the story was read in a much later time, we are turning to another type of evidence altogether. In this sense a *practical* distinction between biblical study and the study of the after-effects of the biblical text can be upheld.

also, the final form of the text has the first importance, and this is likely to be still more widely accepted with the influence both of 'redaction criticism' and of structuralism. The form as it stands is, from the point of view of the tradition, the definitive form, the state in which the tradition ceased to modify the text and agreed that it should stand. Thus both the theological motivation of the tradition and the scholarly techniques of modern investigation agree in according a certain fundamental character to the final state of the text.

I have illustrated this from an Old Testament example, but very similar sequences could be found with, for instance, the stories of Jesus and their successive modes of function as they pass through various stages of oral tradition, stand in a source like Q or Mark, and find a final place and function in Matthew or Luke.

(*k*) Among all matters of selection and ordering within the totality of scripture one stands out as of special importance: the relation between the Old Testament and the New. Old-fashioned ideas which regarded all of the Bible as of equal weight gave, among other things, a stable position to the Old Testament; and this was true, within some limits, of the modern revival of biblical authority, in which so strong a part was played by Hebrew thought. Increasing modern freedom of thought about biblical authority has been accompanied, not necessarily but certainly in fact, by some particular questioning of the value and importance of the Old Testament.[12] In agreeing that theology must use a selecting and ordering process in its relation to the Bible, are we allowing the possibility of a drastic downgrading of the Old Testament in relation to the New?

In the first place it should be remembered that this problem is not a modern one, produced by free-thinking attitudes towards the Bible. An element of critical selection and ordering in the use of the Old Testament was imposed by the structure of Christianity from the beginning, is incorporated within the New Testament documents, and was accepted even by very conservative biblicistic people. Even those who thought women must wear hats in church because it was commanded in the Bible did not obey the entire law of Moses, though that also was commanded in the Bible; at the most they obeyed a precarious selection from within

[12] See in particular my article 'The Old Testament and the New Crisis of Biblical Authority', *Interpretation* xxv (1971), pp. 24–40.

the requirements of that law. All Christian use of the Old Testament has been made somewhat indirect because the relation of the New Testament to the Old is itself a dialectical one.

The case is thus a paradoxical one. Conservative Christians, who regarded the Old Testament as equal in authority with the New, had of necessity to maintain towards it a selectivity which they could not well support in principle. Conversely, the popular 'progressive' arguments against the Old Testament, which commonly cite the moral shockingness of the destruction of the Canaanites, or the unforgiving ethos of the imprecatory Psalms, make sense only on the assumption of a quite fundamentalistic directness of interpretation and application. These arguments make sense only if it is assumed that the reading of something in the Bible can only be a token of universal approbation, so that modern Christians are being invited to delight directly in the killing of ancient Canaanites or to regard the dropping of babies from city walls as an inherently desirable action. No one today however seriously holds these assumptions. Moral judgments by the modern reader are entirely proper, but can be usefully made only after he has examined the background for such stories or poems, the sociology of the period, the question whether the stories are historically true, the reasons why they are told in this form, and the theological arguments within the Israelite tradition which they are used to sustain.[13] Only then can one consider the response – subtle, complicated and far from obvious – which is appropriate for the modern reader. I can however fully sympathize with those who hold that passages of this type should not be used for purely liturgical reading or singing; for, without proper elucidation and interpretation, and used in the celebratory atmosphere of liturgy, they can indeed make a quite indecent impression.

Returning to the more general question, however, I have already published a study of the relation between Old and New Testaments[14] and do not wish to go over the ground again here. For our present question, the fundamental position I would maintain is as

---

[13] Von Rad's basic *Der heilige Krieg im alten Israel* (Zurich, 1951) is not available in English; see perhaps W. Eichrodt, *Theology of the Old Testament* I (London: SCM Press, 1961), pp. 139ff.; J. Pedersen, *Israel III–IV* (London: OUP, 1947), pp. 1–32, for modern treatments of the Israelite attitude to war.

[14] In *Old and New in Interpretation.*

follows. The Christian faith stands equally upon the basis of the Old Testament and of the New or, more correctly, upon the basis of the God of Israel and of Jesus of Nazareth. In this sense the importance of Old and New Testaments is in principle more or less equal; and the two have a certain independence, an independence warranted by the newness of that which took place in Jesus. If there is, then, a process of selecting and ordering within scripture, it is a process of selecting and ordering within the Old Testament and also within the New. But the separation and incomparability of the two is such that the placing of Old and New Testament materials on one scale of higher and lower does not make good sense. If one goes further still and subordinates the Old Testament in principle to the New, or reduces it entirely to something like the status of a merely historical prolegomena to the New, then the effect of this is a shift to a completely different understanding of what Christianity is. Such a subordination or reduction of the status of the Old Testament is no longer preventible by the antecedent exercise of mere authority; it has to be met by looking critically at the eventual output of a theology which thus diminishes the status of the Old Testament.

Nevertheless the function of Old Testament materials within Christian theology would seem to be different in kind from that of New Testament materials. Relevant considerations include the following:

(i) The social setting of the Old Testament, as the document of a national group, is markedly distinct from that of the New.

(ii) The New Testament, being the later in succession, is inclusive of the Old in a way in which the Old is not inclusive of the New; its theology includes throughout reactions to, and reinterpretations and restatements of, Old Testament materials. It produces therefore a 'bi-testamental' view which is lacking in the Old Testament.

(iii) This means that much of the overt theology of the New Testament can feed more directly into the totality of Christian theology than Old Testament materials can.[15]

---

[15] One might add that the production of overt theology at all is something more characteristic of the New Testament; and within Judaism the status and importance of theology as such has always been less certain than in Christianity, which could be a correct consequence of the differences between the Old Testament and the New themselves.

To sum this up, we can consider the question whether the Old Testament and the New are of equal and independent status, or whether alternatively the Old Testament has its status within Christianity only through derivation by way of the New Testament.[16] In my view, the status of the two Testaments is independent for Christian faith, which rests upon the God of Israel and upon Jesus of Nazareth; and if for Christians Jesus is the finality and the culmination, which might place the New Testament in the higher position, Jesus himself stands under the God of Israel, which might place the Old Testament in the higher. The indirectness of the functioning of much Old Testament material does not imply a status basically derivative from the New Testament.

Finally, however, the position outlined above would have to be modified again if we were to consider with favour the position, now not unimportant in the discussion, that the life and teaching of Jesus, though now lying within the New Testament, belonged in actuality rather within the frame of Israel than that of the church, and rather therefore, to use the traditional terms, within the Old Testament than within the New.[17] This however I shall not pursue in itself. But in terms of the general position taken up in this book it should be clear that the traditional formulations of the canon and its boundaries are not absolute. The canonical books themselves go back to the traditions of earlier stages from which they were formed; and these traditions lie within continuities which are not represented by the sharp boundaries of the books and sections of the canon.

[16] See discussion in *Louvain 1971*, p. 19. Incidentally, we can no longer have confidence in the traditional stock argument in favour of the Old Testament, namely the argument that any opposition to it is a form of Marcionitism. Marcionitism is a world-denying position, but modern doubters of the value of the Old Testament are rather world-affirmers. See *Interpretation* xxv (1971), pp. 32–8.

[17] Such a position is akin to Bultmann's in his *Theology of the New Testament*. This position, if right, would affect all sorts of things. For instance, it might suggest that Jesus' teaching about marriage and divorce was addressed to the situation within Israel and did not have within its scope 'Christian marriage' within a Christian church (and state?). This matter of marriage and divorce is incidentally of general interest, since it seems to be the outstanding instance where biblical legalism has been stronger within the Catholic (both Roman and Anglican) than the Protestant wings of the church. The ordination of women is another such case.

X

WORD AND MEANING, LETTER AND SPIRIT

I propose to conclude this study with some consideration of the terms 'verbal' or 'literal' in relation to scriptural interpretation. This will take us back over some ground which has already been discussed, and thus help us in summing up; it will provide some necessary clarification; and it will bring us back in the end to traditional terms like 'verbal inspiration' and the question of the best way in which the status of the Bible may be expressed.

Let us begin with 'literal'. This word is freely used in remarks about the use of the Bible, and yet one seldom sees or hears it analysed. As soon as we analyse it, we observe that this same term is used in quite opposite senses; used in one connection, it means something favourable, while in another connection it means something unfavourable.

In average English speech about the Bible, the word 'literal' suggests fundamentalism; indeed, the average person, asked to define a fundamentalist, will say that he is someone who 'takes the Bible literally'. This however is far from an exact description. The point of conflict between fundamentalists and others is not over *literality* but over *inerrancy*. The typical fundamentalist insistence is not that the Bible must be interpreted literally but that it must be so interpreted as not to admit that it contains error. In order to avoid imputing error to the Bible, fundamentalists twist and turn back and forward between literal and non-literal (symbolic, metaphoric, transferred) exegesis.

To take one of the best-known instances, conservative evangelical opinion today does not follow a literal interpretation of the Genesis creation story. A literal interpretation would be that the world was created in six days, these days being the first of the series which we still experience as days and nights. Modern conservative evangelicals, however, commonly maintain that the six days are six geological ages; another view is that they are six stages, not in the actual creation itself, but in the *revelation* of the truth of creation. It is thus only very extreme fundamentalists who assert that a completely literal interpretation of the six days is obligatory. A symbolic or allegorical interpretation is preferred.[1]

The reason for this preference is plain: a fully literal interpretation would mean a crisis of credibility and a consequent admission of error in the Bible. In order to avoid this, the conservative evangelical interpreter moves over to a non-literal exegesis; only this will save the *inerrancy* of the Bible.

A sensitivity to this can be observed within conservative evangelical theology itself. Thus D. M. Beegle, in a review of R. K. Harrison's *Introduction to the Old Testament*, writes:

> One of the main reasons why Harrison can live with the term 'infallibility' is that he resorts to 'symbolic' interpretation whenever the going gets rough. He takes the Book of Exodus and Book of Numbers enumerations of the Israelites leaving Egypt as 'symbols of relative power, triumph, importance and the like, . . . not meant to be understood either strictly literally or as extant in a corrupt textual form.'[2]

This is exactly the same point which I have been making in the last paragraphs. The typical conservative evangelical exegesis is

[1] This can be substantiated from representative conservative evangelical works such as those published by the Inter-Varsity Fellowship. Cf. for instance *The New Bible Commentary* (2nd edn., 1954), p. 77 (E. F. Kevan): there are 'serious difficulties' in taking them as ordinary days, i.e. taking 'day' literally. 'Others' take them as 'days of dramatic vision, the story being presented to Moses in a series of revelations spread over six days'. A view held by 'many', and apparently the one most approved by the author, is that each 'day' represents 'a geological age'. *The New Bible Dictionary* (1962), art. 'Creation', pp. 271f. (J. A. Thompson), also departs from a literal interpretation and says that the passage is not concerned with chronology: 'Gn. i has an artificial literary structure and is not concerned to provide a picture of chronological sequence but only to assert the fact that God made everything.'

[2] *Interpretation* xxiv (1970), p. 526. Dr Beegle is regarded as an example of 'the new conservatism' by W. Hordern in his chapter on 'The New Face of Conservatism', pp. 83–88.

literal, but only up to a point; when the point is reached where literal interpretation would make the Bible appear to be 'wrong', a sudden switch to non-literal interpretation is made. Thus literal interpretation is not a universal fundamentalist characteristic; conversely, those who say that the Bible 'should not be taken literally' are not necessarily so far from fundamentalism as they think they are.

There is another very good reason, which is not commonly observed, why fundamentalist interpretation is not always literal: biblical source criticism, the operation which detected J, E, D and P, the very critical method which fundamentalist opinion so detests, is also the result of 'taking the Bible literally'. It was just because they took the texts literally that the critics broke through the screen of ancient harmonizing and allegorizing interpretations and reached a position where it became more natural to reconstruct differing sources behind the present biblical books. For example, to cite an old instance, if one takes the Genesis story 'literally', Ishmael was a small child when Hagar was driven into the wilderness; Abraham 'put him on her shoulder' (21.14) and later when she was exhausted she 'threw' or 'thrust' the child under a bush (21.15). But Gen. 17.25 shows that Ishmael was already thirteen years old before Isaac was born. If one takes the text literally, a critical separation of sources becomes very natural. The genealogical material of ch. 17 (P) was written independently of the personal story about Hagar and does not fit with it. Observation of hundreds of such discrepancies, patiently pieced together over a long period, and valued as evidence precisely because the scholars did not allow defensive and harmonizing interpretations to push aside the literal sense of the text, led to the critical reconstruction. In order to avoid this, conservative evangelicals offer an apologetic explanation, the purpose of which is to make the story true as a narrative (or, rather, to make the two narrative units agree into one harmonious story) by avoiding the consequences of the literal sense.[3] Fundamentalist biblical interpretation is forced to apply

---

[3] Cf. again *The New Bible Commentary*, p. 93: 'There is no need to suppose any inconsistency here with the other parts of Genesis, or to imagine this boy of seventeen being carried by his mother like an infant in arms . . . the growing youth would collapse . . . sooner than the physique of the mother who had become accustomed to the desert life . . . Hagar did her best to support him, but at last could hold him up no

such harmonizing apologetics all over the Bible, in order to paper over the cracks left behind by the diversity of sources; and the importance attached to this defensive process greatly damages its theological sensitivity. Literality, then, is only in part a fundamentalist characteristic; it is also an ingredient in critical scholarship. In fundamentalism a higher place is given to the principles of inerrancy and of harmony than to that of literality.

With this argument, then, I hope to have cracked open the common misconception that concern for the literal form of the Bible is a fundamentalist position; and this liberates us for a more open consideration of the literal and the verbal in scriptural interpretation.

The use of 'literal' may be analysed as follows:

The normal use of 'literal' is referential in scope (point A of our triangle, p. 61). We are thinking about the entities or referents to which the text refers. To understand the text literally is to suppose that the referents are just as is stated in the text, the language of the text being understood in a direct sense. It is of this direct and referential interest that people are thinking when they say that fundamentalists 'take the Bible literally'. If it says that Jesus walked on water, then he walked on water; if it says that Methuselah lived for 969 years, then he did live for 969 years.[4] The linguistic terms 'walk on', 'live for', 'water' and 'year' are taken in the same directness and normality as when we say that 'John sits on a chair' or 'he slept for eight hours'.

'Literal' in this sense can be opposed to 'allegorical'. Allegory is also referential in its scope; the difference is that the referent is other than that suggested by the direct sense of the language,

---

longer.' Whatever one thinks of a boy of seventeen being 'supported' by his mother, the explanation is certainly much less *literal* than the source-critical one. I do not think anyone could read the passage without being sure that the natural sense is of a small child.

[4] In this case *The New Bible Commentary* (pp. 82f.) does take a literal view; suggestions that figures like Methuselah were tribes and not individuals, that the years were shorter, that the figures were mystical, are 'attempts to avoid the plain meaning of the passage'. In fact, it seems, 'the fathers of the human race were endowed with longevity, and this may have been according to divine purpose in His providential government of the race.' So also the *New Bible Dictionary*, which seems to treat these figures solemnly as straight biographical data.

being in fact known only by an indirect process working from hints and hidden signals in the language. When the Bible tells of Abraham coming out from Ur of the Chaldees, and an interpreter says that this means the soul departing from the world of the flesh, the referent is now that departure of the soul. The approach is still referential but the referent found by the interpretation is different. Where the text in question is a historical text, the literal interpretation may also be called the historical sense. In an instance like this one, most of us today would regard the literal and historical sense as the right one. In fact the assertion of the primacy of the literal or historical sense in such cases has been an immensely liberating influence in the history of exegesis; this is commonly forgotten or ignored by those who say that it is wrong to 'take the Bible literally'.

However, allegory of the type instanced above can now be generally considered as a thing of the past. What is more likely in modern circumstances is a referential interpretation with a good deal of *vagueness* about it. Stories like those of the Ascension or the Resurrection do have a referent behind them, real entities and real events, and these form the basic sense and value of the stories; but the referents are not exactly as would appear from the direct sense of the language in them. There is some similarity and some difference; people are not sure where exactly to locate them. A literal interpretation would demand a much greater correspondence between the language of the reports and the entities or events referred to.

A common variation of this is a conflict between a more *detailed* and a more *general* interpretation. To cite once again the Genesis creation story, an understanding that would be regarded as literal is commonly in fact a detailed one; that is to say, the various detailed stages, the successive days and the works done on them, are taken as indicative of independent referents following in the same sequence. A more general interpretation would say that 'the story as a whole' had as its reference the creation of the world by God; the details of the story are part of the literary embellishment, all of which however serves only to clarify and reinforce the statement of this one general point (or, perhaps, two or three general points).[5]

[5] Note the adoption of the general interpretation in *The New Bible Dictionary*, cited above, p. 169 n. 1: 'concerned . . . only to assert the fact that God made everything'.

A similar problem is well known in the interpretation of the Gospel parables: is there one referent for the whole story of the Good Samaritan, or does each detail, down to the ass, the inn-keeper and the fee paid to him, have its separate referent?[6]

Two final points to add to the exposé above:

(i) 'Literal' and 'allegorical' can be contrasted, and rightly; but allegorical interpretation commonly coexists with a very minute interest in the detailed verbal form of the text, from which hints for the allegorical understanding are gained. Thus allegory has often been practised by interpreters with a very strong doctrine of verbal inspiration.

(ii) The motives for preferring a literal as against a non-literal exegesis, or vice versa, so long as we remain concerned with referential meaning, are very various. One may mention: (a) a historical sense (it is really significant that Abraham simply departed from Ur); (b) apologetic problems (people can't really walk on water); (c) theological-moral problems (God can't really have done what the literal text says he did, because this would be unworthy of God; therefore a non-literal explanation is necessary – an argument common in the great allegorists like Origen); (d) a legal-ethical sense (God does not just command something to be done by men; rather, his command is a symbol of a deeper educational or edifying intent).

In general, then, we see that even on the referential level alone the understanding and the valuation of the *literal* is something very complex. But when we turn to the study of the intention of the authors, and of the form of the existing text as a literary document (points B and C of our triangle) we find a new series of distinctions.

In exploration of the thoughts, intentions and theologies of the biblical writers, as we have seen, we are working in a different way. The verbal form of the text is being used as evidence from which the mind and circumstances of the writers and traditionists is reconstructed. Considerations which may be valid for any purely referential use of the Bible may now be reversed, or may become entirely irrelevant. The question is not whether Jesus walked on water, but why the Gospel tradition depicted him as walking on

[6] See *Old and New in Interpretation*, pp. 106f.; C. H. Dodd, *The Parables of the Kingdom* (London: Nisbet, 1935), pp. 11f. In New Testament study it has become common to call it *parable* if the general interpretation is intended, *allegory* if the detailed is intended.

water; it is not whether Methuselah lived for 969 years, but why the writer of Genesis was interested in him and why he put down 969 years as his age at death (or, correspondingly, why the Samaritan Hebrew text put it down as 720); it is not whether Jesus ascended to heaven, but what place this ascension has in the theology of the writers who mention it.

When we look at things in this way, we immediately see that the verbal form of the text assumes much greater positivity and importance. Even on the referential level it had, as we have seen, much more positive importance than is usually supposed, for instance in its acting as the base for the historical sense in narrative passages (as against the allegorical sense), and in its acting as the base for critical historical reconstruction. But on the intentional level, working towards the minds of the tradition and of the writers, its positive importance is even greater. If the Genesis writer followed a certain pattern in alternating the verbs 'God created' (*bara'*) and 'God made' (*'aśa*); if he constructed a careful and schematic account of creation in one week, ending up with the Sabbath, and patterning the various deeds of creation over the different days; if he was interested enough in the ages of the antediluvians like Methuselah to provide detailed figures for their lives; if he did all these things, we can be sure that he had a reason for doing them, that this reason is a deep-set part of his theology and a profound element in his character as a writer; and we can be sure that we have no clues for the discovery of his theology and his character as a writer other than these very patterns of verbal behaviour which I have listed, plus a thousand others like them.

This fact in turn is a main reason for the technical concern of biblical scholarship with the details of language, illustrated in the grammars of Hebrew and Greek, the concordances, the dictionaries, the monographs discussing patterns of parallelism and verse-structure, the word counts, and so on. The detailed verbal evidence is the route to the mind of the writer.

Let us keep to our example of the story of creation. There are at least two quite separate questions here. One is: what do we affirm about the creation of the world (referential)? The other is: what was the theological intention of the Genesis writer (intentional or historical)? In order to fulfil the study of the latter question, we have to take seriously all sorts of things which on the former level may possibly be left aside. We certainly have to take very seriously the six-day scheme, because it is so evidently central to the writer's intention; but this is quite a different matter from supposing that there is in the actual external world and its history some real event or process corresponding to this scheme. In other words, there are many things in the Bible which are vital for exegesis which nevertheless are not supposed by us to represent external entities or events. Moreover, we today in general do not move directly from biblical texts to external referents, but from biblical texts to the theological intentions of the writers and only from there indirectly to external referents. Thus the modern interpretative pattern is seldom or never a direct referential relation between the text and the entities referred to.

Within the pattern of modern exegesis, therefore, the idea that one should not 'take the Bible literally' has become an anachronism. It has meaning only within a simply referential framework of study. In this respect it belongs together with a literal fundamentalism. Those who say 'we don't take the Bible literally' tend to imply that the Bible does give a correct referential picture, but only if the language is not taken directly. What is more correct to say is something like this: our understanding of the writer is based on the detailed linguistic form of his text, but what we believe is another matter, involving a further and more complicated series of considerations.

To put it negatively: the idea of avoiding literal interpretation, which within an antique and purely referential framework appears to be rather open, free and sophisticated, actually becomes an obstacle to the discovery procedures of modern sophisticated exegesis. Modern exegesis, with its interest directed towards the mind and the theology of the biblical writer and the tradition behind him (point B of our triangle) or towards the forms, patterns and images of the existing text (point C), works through a close observation of the linguistic form of the text. The problem therefore is that of the difference between a *generalized* and a *particular* interpretation of the Bible. I shall take my stand definitely on the side of the particular interpretation. As we have suggested in the preceding argument, reservations about a literal interpretation, in themselves reasonably justified when applied on a referential level, tend when applied to modern exegesis to produce a generalized interpretation, where the detail of the text is brushed aside and global assertions about the meaning of the whole are made.

'Taken as a whole', we are told, a passage means such and such a thing; it 'basically adds up to' one simple point. Simplifying and generalizing exegesis of this kind must be familiar to all who listen to sermons.

In favour of the particular approach the following may be urged:

(*a*) All our argument has emphasized the importance of the *differences* between one biblical writer and another, one tradition and another.[7] It is these which give the real bite, the peculiar savour, to the variety within the Bible. The same incident, as narrated in Matthew, Mark and Luke, may have only slight differences of wording; but these small differences are tokens of the fact that the incident is within each Gospel part of a quite different total theological outlook.

(*b*) Any passage, moreover, can be seen and interpreted differently according to the various stages and levels of the tradition at which it is seen. This militates against the making of generalized statements of meaning.

(*c*) These facts about the variety of the biblical material, the many-sidedness with which it can be seen, are a reason for its richness and inexhaustibility as a food for the thought and meditation of the church. More accurate theological statements can no doubt be made; but these no more replace the Bible in its functions within worship than a commentary on Shakespeare's plays can replace the plays themselves as a dramatic text.

(*d*) I do not suggest that generalizations about the Bible, or general statements about parts of it, cannot be made. But they can be usefully made only on the basis of fresh reappraisal of the particularities of the texts. What tends to happen is the reverse: general impressions about the sense of biblical passages tend to be passed on from one generation to another and to blanket out any real quest after the true meaning of the passages.

(*e*) It may be objected that an emphasis on the particularity of the texts is only an invitation to a pedantic grubbing among details. This is not so. For one thing, I do not suggest that all particularities, all differences in detail, have theological significance. Some are accidental or non-distinctive. Pedantry comes not from attention to detail, but from the seeing of detail within the wrong framework, or from the mindless attribution of equal significance to all details.

[7] Cf. above, p. 99.

Discrimination between detail that is significant and detail that is not significant is achieved not by a flight into generality but by properly guided experience in the handling of detail.

These points only bring us to two more important theological points which lie at the heart of this question:

(*a*) The tendency toward a generalizing interpretation belongs to a way of thinking in which theological and moral assertions must as far as possible take the form of general and universal principles. Modern appreciation of the Bible, however, has rightly emphasized that its mode of thought and presentation is seldom compatible with this kind of universality.

(*b*) It may be objected in Pauline terms that 'the letter killeth, but the Spirit maketh alive'. But this is just what that Pauline declaration does not mean. It is not a declaration against the guidance of the verbal form of the text and in favour of generalized statements of meaning. Paul is not talking about the difference between literal and non-literal, or particular and generalized, interpretation of Christian scripture; he is speaking about the contrast between the operation of the Jewish law and the operation of the Spirit (cf. NEB: 'for the written law condemns to death, but the Spirit gives life'). The long tradition, in which this Pauline sentence has been used to excuse all sorts of 'spiritualizing' interpretation, is quite unjustified. If the text had in fact had this sort of question in mind, it would have been more proper to say that 'the letter giveth life'.[8] Or, as I myself would put it, the verbal form of the Bible does not stand in contrast with its meaning, but is the indicator of that meaning; or, more theologically, it is not in conflict with the 'Spirit' which is the presence of God accompanying the reading, but is in accord with that Spirit.

[8] Something similar is the emphasis of J. Wirsching's recent book. Cf. for example his summary statement on p. 230: 'Scripture is nothing other than the letter of the Bible, in so far as it always seeks anew to become "Spirit" and in fact always anew becomes "Spirit".' Again, 'The "Spirit", which the biblical letter always seeks anew to become, is historical like the letter itself . . . it is something thoroughly incomprehensible and illimitable, so that no one can get a grasp of it; but it is also "literal" spirit, plunged deep in the separative tensions of historical existence, and it is within them an entirely human form of expression, which has constantly to be tested (I John 4.1) and to be distinguished from other forms of spirit (I Cor. 12.10).' The reader should bear in mind that in Wirsching's usage 'scripture' and 'Bible' are not identical: the Bible has to 'become' scripture. Cf. above, p. 20 n.

On the basis of all these considerations we are now able to recognize that theological assertions about the status of the Bible can quite properly be assertions about its verbal or linguistic form. Its linguistic form, far from being something antithetical to its 'real meaning', is the means by which the meaning is conveyed; it is the criterion by which we test all interpretations which claim to state the meaning. The basic principle of interpretation is: why was it said in this way, and not in some other way? The linguistic form of the text is not a jumble of dead symbols from which by some process of decipherment meaning has to be extracted; it is the expression of meaning.

It is therefore not unreasonable that the older theologians spoke about inspiration as 'verbal', even though our thinking has veered far away from theirs. In so far as this was connected with ideas of divine dictation of each word, or of inerrancy in every detail, our thoughts have gone in quite the opposite direction. This being so, however, we no longer have any good reason to be shy about including a reference to the verbal form of the Bible in any assertions we make about its status as a whole. The quest for a formulation which will do justice to the status of the Bible but avoid the connotations of the word 'verbal', such as *plenary inspiration*, inspiration of the *ideas*, inspiration of the *authors*, inspiration of the *inner theology*, and so on, is just no longer important. What we know about the authors, the ideas, the inner theology and so on is known ultimately from the verbal form of the Bible. As in any other literary work, the verbal form is its mode of communicating meaning. If the verbal form of the Bible were different, then its meaning would be different.[9]

[9] The Protestant scholastic theologians maintained that even the vowel points of the Hebrew biblical text were divinely inspired, and this opinion has often been regarded as the ultimate and crowning absurdity of all theories of inspiration. But, as I remarked long ago (*SJT* xi [1958], p. 92), the idea is in some ways a sensible one and indeed, within the terms of the then discussion, perhaps the only logical one. The old Hebrew script registered only certain segments of the verbal form of the Bible (roughly speaking, all consonants unambiguously, and some vowels optionally and ambiguously). The full linguistic form was until late times known, but was carried in oral tradition; the vowel points (added about AD 600–900) were a graphic registration of this oral tradition. The late registration of the vowel points is to us an oddity; but in fact it stands in good continuity with the ancient Israelite movement of tradition as a whole. Of course, the old

Since these thoughts have brought us back to terms like 'verbal inspiration', it may be proper to look back, from the end of our study, at the discussion we earlier had of various terms like 'inspiration' and 'authority'. The construction of 'inspiration' which to me seems possible has already been set out;[10] and in some ways the term fits well with the basic position which has been adopted in this book. The major question, however, is the practical one, whether there is any hope of using the term 'inspiration' for the position here adopted, when the entire popular acceptation of the word is in terms of inerrancy and infallibility. It is possible indeed that a programme of instruction along the lines of 'a scripture inspired but fallible' might alter the popular acceptation. It would, incidentally, do some good of another kind: for undoubtedly many people hold the view that God, by the mere fact of being God, cannot say anything imperfect, just as they think that he cannot change (the concept of God, analytically, implying unchangeability). The breakdown of this particular popular view of God would be good for Christian faith in many ways.[11] But whether any of this is likely to happen is very doubtful.

As for the term 'Word of God', we have not pursued this very far. That one may, from a practical point of view, preface the reading of scripture with a phrase such as 'Hear the Word of God' seems quite appropriate, and is a good tradition in many churches. Under the terms of the discussion in this book, it would mean that the Bible, a crystallization of the tradition of God's people, is made by him into the vehicle of his own speech to succeeding genera-

---

theologians also meant that the points were without error, which we could not accept today; but from the point of view of their function as determiners of meaning their high importance as part of the biblical text is quite justified. On this in general see my 'Reading a Script without Vowels', forthcoming in the Mont Follick Lecture series (Manchester University Press).

[10] See above, pp. 130ff.

[11] This completely static view of God is in conflict with the biblical insistence on the living God; it makes it difficult for people to see theological significance in what happens in the world; and it is a major obstacle to the appreciation of the Bible in any modern categories. Against this static view it is preferable to say, even at the risk of being misunderstood, that God has a history – though, naturally, not identical with human history. So below, p. 181.

tions of that people.[12] But this understanding is a fairly vague one, and those who have used Word-of-God terminology have generally had to fall back, for their more precise judgments, either upon 'inspiration' or upon rather complicated structures of the Barthian type. We cannot expect the term 'Word of God' to be very effective in the present fluid discussion.

For the placing of scripture in any scheme of priorities, for expressing the grading of it above, below or beside such other influences as might bear upon the mind of the church, 'authority' is the best-adapted term. But, as we have seen, it is doubtful whether 'authority' represents, or fits in with, the effective functioning structure of modern theology.[13] The term can continue to be used, if it is used loosely and draws its connotations from the sort of structures which existed in theology in an earlier stage; but to define it rigorously and to apply it as a binding force on all the variety of modern theological thinking seems a possibility of doubtful value.

The other concept which we mentioned initially, that of *function*, itself functions in a different way. One cannot say that the Bible has a function and leave it at that; compared with saying that the Bible is inspired or that it has authority, this is an empty concept; and this may be part of its value. To give content to functional descriptions, we have to take separately the work of historical scholars, of literary critics, of theologians, of preachers and so on. Talk about the functions of the Bible in such different kinds of work does not have the imposingness, the apparent strength, of concepts like authority; it does not sound as if it will bring anyone into conformity. But it has two advantages. First of all, since the processes concerned are common property to most or all currents of theology, it might bring improved understanding; and understanding, I have said, is really now our concern, rather than authority. Secondly, it has diversity. This diversity seems to fit with the many diverse modes of operation of the human under-

---

[12] I wrote in *SJT* xi (1958), p. 92: 'Could it not be said that God . . . calls forth the Word of his People, Israel and the church, in a response of witness and of worship, and this Word coalesces in the scripture? But for following ages God makes that Word of his people his own Word.' But the review from which this is taken includes some ideas which I have now abandoned.

[13] Cf. above, pp. 28, 113ff., 162.

standing in the study of the Bible. Beyond this, it means that we need no longer strive to bring our assertions about the status of the Bible under the umbrella of one guiding concept. It has not in fact proved necessary in the writing of this book to make a definite choice between them. The content of the individual questions has proved more important and more rewarding.

In our last word we shall return to the 'unity' of the Bible. We have considered on the one hand the possibility of seeing the Bible as one, whether through a literary study of the final form of the whole or through the discernment of a basic underlying skeleton of common concepts; and we have on the other hand rather emphasized the diversities and particularities of the Bible, seeing it not as a communication of true theological information but as a struggle, a conflict, a controversy, in which men came into combat with one another over their God. In saying this we should not underestimate the common elements which exist within the Bible and hold it together; and we should not underestimate the degree to which future study may bring us to comprehend its unity more deeply.[14] But the profoundest unity is not a unity *within* the Bible, on the level of its common patterns of thought, or consisting in a balance we may discern between its different emphases, between its conflicting viewpoints; it is rather the unity of the one God, which also is a unity within a variety, and – dare we say? – a unity with a history. The use within the church of a book so diverse as the Bible must imply a conviction that ultimately all this diversity will not lead off into totally irreconcilable opposites. Such a conviction, however, does not necessarily have to be comprehended now by us, or to be expressed in studies, in books and documents, as something we now perceive; its realization belongs rather to faith and to hope.

[14] Cf. above, p. 99.

ABBREVIATIONS

BJRL   *Bulletin of the John Rylands Library*

BSOAS *Bulletin of the School of Oriental and African Studies*

IDB   *Interpreter's Dictionary of the Bible* (4 vols., New York, 1962)

JTS   *Journal of Theological Studies*

RThPh *Revue de Théologie et de Philosophie*

SEÅ   *Svensk Exegetisk Årsbok*

SJT   *Scottish Journal of Theology*

BIBLIOGRAPHY

This is only a simple bibliography of the subject, and is mainly confined to works in English. It does not include all works cited in this book, but only those more relevant to the subject as a whole.

It may be helpful if from the total list I select a few works which are available and which can be recommended for those wishing to pursue the subject further, perhaps in discussion groups; I would then recommend:

Short Guide for Further Study

a. The Study Outline by J. Barr and others, 'The Authority of the Bible', in *Ecumenical Review* xxi.

b. The Faith and Order report, *Louvain 1971*.

c. The January 1971 number of *Interpretation* (Richmond, Virginia) containing articles by Barr, Ladd, Robinson, Murphy, Peter, Kaufman and Ritschl. This number formed the basis of a colloquium at Richmond in February 1971.

d. L. Hodgson and others, *On the Authority of the Bible* (articles by Hodgson, Evans, Burnaby, Ebeling and Nineham).

e. C. F. Evans, *Is 'Holy Scripture' Christian?*

f. D. E. Nineham, 'The Use of the Bible in Modern Theology' (copies can be bought from the John Rylands Library, Deansgate, Manchester).

g. B. Vawter, *Biblical Inspiration*, for a Roman Catholic approach.

Fuller bibliographical details are given in the lists below, where these works are included again.

1. Ecumenical documents

Richardson, A., and Schweitzer, W., *Biblical Authority for Today* (London: SCM Press, 1951) – a collection of essays on different themes and from different ecclesiastical points of view; includes on pp. 240–44 the report of the Wadham Conference (1949) on 'Guiding Principles for the Interpretation of the Bible'.

New Directions in Faith and Order: Bristol 1967 (Geneva: World Council of Churches, 1968. Faith and Order Paper no. 50). See pp. 32–41: 'The Significance of the Hermeneutical Problem for the Ecumenical Movement'; discussion and reports on this, pp. 106f., 151f.

Barr, J., and others, 'The Authority of the Bible: a Study Outline', *The Ecumenical Review* xxi (no. 2, April, 1969), 135–66.

Louvain 1971 (Geneva: World Council of Churches, 1971. Faith and Order Paper no. 59). See 'The Authority of the Bible', pp. 9–23; discussion, pp. 212–15

2. Books and articles on the status of the Bible in general

Barr, J., Review of J. K. S. Reid, *The Authority of Scripture*, *SJT* xi (1958), pp. 86–93
— *Old and New in Interpretation* (London: SCM Press, 1966)
Bruce, F. F. and Rupp, E. G., edd., *Holy Book and Holy Tradition* (Manchester: Manchester University Press, 1968). A work containing essays on the situation in a variety of different religions.
Campenhausen, H. F. von, *Die Entstehung der christlichen Bibel* (Tübingen: Mohr, 1968)
Cunliffe-Jones, H., *The Authority of the Biblical Revelation* (London: Clarke, 1945)
Dodd, C. H., *The Authority of the Bible* (2nd edition, London: Fontana, 1960; first published 1929)
Evans, C. F., 'The Inspiration of the Bible', in Hodgson, *Authority*, pp. 25–32; originally in *Theology* lix (1956), pp. 11–17
— 'Bible and Tradition', ibid., pp. 69–79; originally in *Theology* lx (1957), pp. 437–44
— *Is 'Holy Scripture' Christian?* (London: SCM Press, 1971)
Gardner, H., *The Business of Criticism* (London: Oxford paperback, 1963; first published, 1959)
Gustavson, J. M., 'The Place of Scripture in Christian Ethics: a methodological Study', *Interpretation* xxiv (1970), pp. 430–55
Hodgson, L. and others, *On the Authority of the Bible* (London:

SPCK, 1960; includes essay 'God and the Bible' by L. Hodgson, and essays by C. F. Evans, D. E. Nineham, et al.

Huxtable, J., *The Bible Says* (London: SCM Press, 1962; Religious Book Club, 148)

Kaufman, G. D., 'What shall we do with the Bible?' *Interpretation* xxv (1971), pp. 95–112

Kelsey, D. H., 'Appeals to Scripture in Theology', *Journal of Religion* xlviii (1968), pp. 1–21

Ladd, G. E., 'The Search for Perspective', *Interpretation* xxv (1971), pp. 41–62

Nineham, D. E., *The Church's Use of the Bible, Past and Present* (London: SPCK, 1963)

— 'Wherein lies the Authority of the Bible?', in Hodgson, *Authority*, pp. 81–96

— 'The Use of the Bible in Modern Theology', in *BJRL* lii (1969), pp. 178–99

Ramsey, A. M., 'The Authority of the Bible', *Peake's Commentary on the Bible* (2nd edition, ed. M. Black and H. H. Rowley; Edinburgh: Nelson, 1962), pp. 1–7

Reid, J. K. S., *The Authority of Scripture* (London: Methuen, 1957)

Richardson, A., *The Bible in an Age of Science* (London: SCM Press, 1961)

Ritschl, D., 'A Plea for the Maxim: Scripture *and* Tradition', *Interpretation* xxv (1971), pp. 113–28

Rowley, H. H., 'The Authority of the Bible', in his *From Moses to Qumran* (London: Lutterworth Press, 1963), pp. 3–31

Smart, J. D., *The Strange Silence of the Bible in the Church* (London: SCM Press, 1970)

Wirsching, J., *Was ist schriftgemäß?* (Gütersloh: Gerd Mohn, 1971)

3. Works on the Position of the Old Testament in particular

Barr, J., 'Tradition and Expectation in Ancient Israel', *SJT* x (1957), pp. 24–34

— 'Den teologiska värderingen av den efterbibliska judendomen', *SEÅ* xxxii (1967), pp. 69–78

— 'Le Judaïsme postbiblique et la théologie de l'Ancient Testament', *RThPh* (1968), pp. 209–17

— 'Judaism – its Continuity with the Bible', the seventh Monte-fiore Memorial Lecture (Southampton University, 1968)

— 'The Old Testament and the New Crisis of Biblical Authority', *Interpretation* xxv (1971), pp. 24–40

Bright, J., *The Authority of the Old Testament* (London: SCM Press, 1967)

Hebert, A. G., *The Authority of the Old Testament* (London: Faber and Faber, 1947)

Lohfink, N., *The Christian Meaning of the Old Testament* (London: Burns and Oates, 1969)

Mowinckel, S., *The Old Testament as Word of God* (Oxford: Blackwell, 1960)

4. Works on the Roman Catholic position in particular

Burtchaell, J. T., *Catholic Theories of Biblical Inspiration since 1810* (Cambridge: CUP, 1969)

Murphy, R. E., and Peter, C. J., 'The Role of the Bible in Roman Catholic Theology', *Interpretation* xxv (1971), pp. 78–94

Rahner, K., *Inspiration in the Bible* (Freiburg: Herder, and Edinburgh: Nelson, 1961)

Tavard, G. H., *Holy Writ or Holy Church* (London: Burns and Oates, 1959)

Vawter, B., *Biblical Inspiration* (London: Hutchinson, 1972)

5. Works on Protestant conservatism and fundamentalism

Hebert, G., *Fundamentalism and the Church of God* (London: SCM Press, 1957)

Hordern, W., 'The New Face of Conservatism', ch. iv of his *New Directions in Theology Today*, Volume I: *Introduction* (London: Lutterworth, 1968), pp. 74–95

Packer, J. I., *'Fundamentalism' and the Word of God* (London: Inter-Varsity Fellowship, 1958)

INDEX